contemporary
design secrets

contemporary
design secrets
the art of building a house in the countryside

jane burnside

photography **chris hill**

BOOKLINK

contents

this book is simply how I do it and why it works

foreword

Jason Orme

Editor *Homebuilding and Renovating*

Well, if you're at the stage where you've picked up a book on commissioning a contemporary style new home in the countryside, it's fair to say that you're not after an easy life. You're braver than the average bear who settles for housing 'off-the-shelf'.

Braver too, even, than those who specify their own homes, but opt for a traditional style that just 'fits in' (although that certainly has its place). I mean, for a start, doesn't the book title sound controversial by default? The juxtaposition of contemporary architecture and the countryside is something that, to many eyes, simply shouldn't happen. Contemporary design, with its clean, straight lines and reliance on modern products and engineering, couldn't exactly blend into rural surroundings. For the layperson to then throw themselves into the process of trying to win planning permission – not to mention ensuring that the home they are committing their lives to is successfully achieved – is, if you think about it, really quite extraordinary.

I first met Jane Burnside ten years ago when, as a cub reporter, I was asked to visit Northern Ireland to check out the work of an emerging and highly-rated young architect with a reputation for creating homes that blended architecturally – exciting exteriors with light, family-orientated, interiors. These houses were clearly a league above the average 'contemporary' home knocking around back then, which were all too often entrenched in copying Modernist styles, to the detriment of instinctive reactions to the unique nature of each and every site.

Over the years since, I've come to appreciate that the two priorities of 'high' architecture and pleasing interiors don't easily meet – in fact, more often than not, they compete. It seems that architects designing contemporary homes don't usually bother with such matters as liveability and light, which get in the way of their grand vision. Jane's homes were, and are, different. Remarkably for the modern homes I'd come across, her homes didn't jar with the landscape, rather, they added to its natural beauty. They were brilliant to look at from the outside and even better to wander around and suffer a bit of owner-envy once you were inside. This book is a welcome chance for everyone else, architects included, to learn how she does it.

All the photographs of contemporary houses in this book are Jane's designs. They show that the secret of a successful, contemporary house in the countryside is to add to the natural landscape, and not detract from it. It's not just about choosing the best view to show off; it's about considering every aspect of the location and designing with the grain of the ground, not against it. The challenges of getting 'contemporary' right – both in terms of its surroundings, and its liveability as a working home – are only to be taken on by those with either exceptional talent or the humility to listen to *you*, the client, as well as learn from what others are doing. Jane is a rare architect in that she combines all of those qualities. Her book is the first of its kind to really get to the heart of equipping ordinary people with enough knowledge to get it right themselves or, more likely, help their own architect get it right.

Reading this book I'm struck time and time again by how important good design is to the creation of a new home. This makes it all the more surprising that good design receives such little attention from many people commissioning individual homes. As a reader, once you've finished this book, you'll have learned a heck of a lot, have realised how much you don't know, and, most importantly of all, be thoroughly energised to go off and create your own contemporary home.

Jason

if your new house benefits from even a dusting of Jane's magic, our landscape will be all the richer

introduction

Designing a contemporary house in the landscape is one of the most exciting adventures you will ever embark upon.

For me, the art of building a house in the countryside is like writing a piece of music. The same notes and instruments are available to everyone, but it is the composer who shapes the piece, releasing its character and mood. So, too, with design. I get enormous pleasure from designing a house and seeing what emerges from under the scaffolding, like a butterfly from its chrysalis. This is the joy of creating a building.

Frank Lloyd Wright, the doyen of early twentieth century American houses, allegedly said there were only so many conversations one could have in a lifetime about a woman's closet. After 20 years, and over 200 clients, some might wonder why I, too, have not had my fill of homes and closets and moved on to public buildings. The truth is I never tire of designing people's homes, and trust I never shall.

All the design challenges that are presented by a public building (such as order, form and light) are also present in domestic buildings: just on a smaller scale. And because I see every new house as a natural progression from previous ones, and because the turn-around period from idea to reality is relatively quick, my focus on houses has enabled me to develop what, I hope, is a distinctive architectural voice. I have sought to express this through a series of timeless, contemporary classics that lie beyond the whims of fashion. This series will, I believe, continue to adapt in response to the growing aspirations of clients and their awareness of environmental issues.

When I lectured in Architecture at Queen's University Belfast, I wanted my students to appreciate that good design is a process. It is also a cyclical process – not a linear one – in which sketches, ideas and aspirations become more refined as you get to grips with more information. Despite growing complexity, and the things that get added along the way, the process should be one of continual simplification. The goal of great design is artful simplicity. This book will give you an understanding of, and guide you through, this design process.

As you journey through this book, you'll discover that being contemporary is not the same thing as being faddish. Contemporary design is not about building wacky spaceships. Instead, being contemporary means drawing on a rich history of architectural influences – from Norman forts to labourers' cottages; Scottish castles to Renaissance villas; and from Irish bawns to Scandinavian eco-houses. Being truly contemporary, means being rooted in the past, yet responding to the present.

So, in this book, we will explore what can be achieved artistically in the countryside. This isn't as grand, or high-flown, as it sounds. It's about creating something that is both practical and beautiful – and that is just what clients want. Ultimately, this book is about empowering people to get the best house they can from their architect.

The time has come to expand the canvas of what we can design in the countryside. Welcome to the world of *Contemporary Design Secrets*!

JANE BURNSIDE

Architect RIBA MRIAI Rome Scholar

Let's expand the canvas of what we can design in the countryside.

1

the house in its landscape

the vision

getting a feel for the rural site

embracing the landscape

the look of the house

the vision

Imagine you are at an event where, instead of a name-card at your table setting, everyone has a cardboard cut-out of their house.

it is interesting – and revealing – how the choices we make in life are reflected in our houses

What do you think that might tell you about the people you are talking to? Would it make a difference to your impression of them? It might subvert a few expectations. You could discover that the statistician, on your right, actually lives in a fabulous pump house, while the well-known politician, on your left, actually lives in a house built by the council.

Wherever we choose to live says something about our life's vision, to some degree. This is especially the case if you are building a bespoke house, where all the choices are effectively yours. So, what is your vision and how can you capture it?

To make a stunning house you only need one really good idea, carried out with complete conviction. Contemporary design is a very broad spectrum. Whatever your vision for your contemporary house, you'll find your ideas fall somewhere along that spectrum, which ranges from perhaps clinical functionality, on the one hand, to possibly a relaxed beach house, on the other. To hone your vision, make a mood board and compile your brief.

make your mood board

Remember that design is a process, moving from complexity to artful simplicity. Mood boards are a key part of this process.

Usually mood boards are prepared by designers, who then present their ideas to their clients. I reverse this sequence. Instead, I ask clients to prepare their mood board by putting onto it all their ideas of what they would like in their house – and, sometimes, even what they don't like. Mood boards enable clients to access and get in touch with what they really want from their new home. They empower clients. Mood boards also allow me to get inside their heads, and really understand what they need me to achieve.

Using a large, A1-sized sheet of card gather images of all the things you love: interiors, furniture, flooring, paintings, gardens, and so on. Try to avoid complete houses because your house should be unique. Don't worry if some images are crazy or if others don't fit together. But do try to work out why one image appeals to you whilst another, seemingly identical one, does not.

Each time I meet with clients to go through their mood board, I am reminded of the great American architect, Robert Stern, who said: "The dialogue between client and architect is about as intimate as any conversation you can have, because when you are talking about building a house, you're talking about dreams." I love going through clients' mood boards. It's one of my favourite parts of the design process because, at this stage, everything is possible. Eventually, after a lot of discussion, an overall sense of the new building will emerge. At this point, we can edit out what is no longer relevant. As I said in the Introduction, design is a cyclical process that involves constant simplification.

Sometimes a zany image will inspire the overall design. I'll never forget the client who came to me with a photograph of a woman showering outside, in front of a steel grain silo. I thought: 'Is he serious? An outside shower in Ireland?' I probed carefully, not wanting to offend, and it turned out he was responding to the 'rawness' of the image. The endpoint of this part of the design process was the Zen House – an essay in natural simplicity. I even designed for him a cylindrical steel-clad shower, off his bedroom, set into a pool in the garden. So be careful what you wish for – you might just get it!

create a mood board with everything you would love in your new home – eventually an overall sense of the new building will emerge

compile your brief

Mood boards address the heart, but you also need facts to design a house!

A compilation of the relevant facts is called the brief, and, for a private house, there are two key parts:

- a schedule of accommodation and
- clients' unique requirements

The schedule of accommodation is simply a list of all the rooms you require, together with their approximate sizes. Your architect will be able to give you approximate build estimates based on cost per square foot. This build estimate will reflect the quality of materials and the complexity of the design. The size of the rooms are then totalled up and a percentage of this sub-total, usually between 10–15%, is added for circulation space (including corridors, stairs etc.) to give a projected total floor area.

Obviously, the higher the estimated area of your house, the higher the cost. Likewise, the quality of materials. The goal is to balance the size and quality of your home with the size of your budget.

To discover clients' unique requirements, I encourage them to think about how they would like to use their physical space on a daily basis. Remember that it's about how you will actually live, not how you think you might like to live. The following questions are a good place to begin:

compile your brief to reflect how you will live – not how you think you might like to live

- How many people will be living in the new home and, if there are children, what ages are they?
- Does a friend or family member have any particular needs regarding health or mobility?
- How does the family operate on a weeknight? Do you have a family meal together? Where do you like the children to do their homework – in their bedrooms or where they can be supervised? Where do you most like to watch television?
- If you entertain, do you need a formal dining room or are you more casual? How many people do you need to entertain at a dining table? How many do you need to seat for a large family get-together?
- Do you need a family room for the children and a living room for the adults?
- Do you work from home? If so, do your clients need to arrive and leave in complete privacy, or, does it not matter if they engage with your family?
- Do you have particular furniture or art pieces that need to be incorporated into the design?
- Do you have any hobbies that need to be designed into the house? Snooker tables and touring caravans can all be accommodated unobtrusively provided they are integrated from the outset.
- How many bedrooms do you need? Do you like to wake up to the sun in the morning?
- How much clothes storage do you need? If you have girls of a similar age, would they enjoy sharing a walk-in dressing area or would that result in a war?
- Do you need a designated guest bedroom?
- How many bathrooms do you need (or want to clean)? Do you need a main bathroom if every bedroom has access to an en suite?
- Will you eat or cook outdoors in the summer? Would you like a BBQ or an outdoor kitchen? Would a covered sitting area be useful?
- What will your garage requirements and garden storage needs be?
- Do you have pets and what are their requirements? Where do they get fed and cleaned? (I have even installed a full flushing w/c into a dog kennel!).

getting a feel for the rural site

When you build your house in the countryside you are adding a permanent object to a landscape shared by others. For me, that's a sobering thought.

build on the worst part of the site – that way you will always have the best part of the site to enjoy

It's a privilege to make a mark on the landscape, so it's vital our impact adds to the scene, and does not detract. The house doesn't have to be invisible – but it does have to be beautiful.

If your first reaction is to build a house in the middle of a field and put a tarmac drive all the way around it, I hope this book will encourage you to have second thoughts!

You can achieve so much by carefully thinking through the design of your house; from the outside to the inside.

The most important steps are the first ones. Design begins with the site.

choose the right site

In County Antrim, Northern Ireland, there used to be an old test for selecting a site: place your cap on your walking stick and then go home for your dinner. If the fairies haven't taken it by the time you return, then it's a fine place to build your house.

Of course, nowadays, we think in terms of microclimate (how the climate of a specific place differs from the climate of the wider context). But it amounts to the same local wisdom. If you place your cap on a walking stick on the top of a hill, the wind (or the fairies!) will quickly whisk it away. This is why traditional rural houses are rarely found on hilltops but nestle, instead, in landscape dips or hunkered down beneath hills.

Even within your site there will be areas of wind and shelter. There are some places you can happily stand and chat, and others from which you naturally retreat. Your innate feelings won't change just because you've put a house there!

I chose to position the Origami House beside an old dam on the farmland. Everyone thought I was building the house in the wrong place and, being country folk, they didn't hold back ("You'll be living with the rats," they warned). It certainly wasn't the most impressive place on the four-acre smallholding. It was almost by the road and it was shaded by trees for most of the day. Nevertheless, it was where my children used to make camp and where we'd picnic in the summer evenings. It had fabulous, long views across the open fields towards the setting sun, and the sound of the waterfall from the dam was idyllic. I trusted my feelings and now everyone tells me how fortunate I was to have had such a wonderful site in the first place! I've learned to accept that as a compliment.

some of the best houses emerge from the most challenging sites

If you have a view from your site, undoubtedly, you'll have the wind too. Don't despair! If you can't find a sheltered place on your site, try to create one. Shape the house to form a courtyard entrance, away from the prevailing wind, and, if your building is small, use garaging, existing mature hedges or stone walls to form the third and fourth sides of the courtyard.

Planning authorities prefer houses to be in sheltered dips, not only because that is where smaller, rural houses used to be located, but also because it is where new houses can most easily be absorbed into the landscape.

Skyline development is rarely permitted but, when it is granted, this is usually because the architect has presented a strong case for the unique. So, don't rule out an elevated position, but do respond to the hilltop setting. Afterall, without breaking skyline we wouldn't have such memorable edifices as Mussenden Temple on the north coast of Ulster or even Edinburgh Castle.

The Hill House, opposite, overlooks the mountains of Mourne in Northern Ireland. This landscape is characterised by drumlins and isolated trees. The traditional farmhouse model sits atop the drumlins in a singular rectangular form with its longest side overlooking the land, and its chimneys on the gable ends. The Hill House radically rotates this model breaking down the mass of the traditional form, through the use of two glazed, gabled pavilions linked together with a glass 'bridge'.

If the house you design is truly born of its context, such that it cannot change its location without losing its significance, then you have succeeded in designing a unique house.

In my view, sites are what you make them. Some of the best houses in the world emerge from the most challenging sites. They force you to work harder and be more creative.

a great building in the landscape is one that makes the landscape more beautiful than it was before the building was present

position rooms to track the sun

It wasn't until the Italian Renaissance that rooms in peoples' houses were designed for a particular purpose.

Before then, people moved around the house, seeking sun or shade, and often took their furniture with them. That's why, until the mid-1700s, rooms were simply designated as being for either 'morning' or 'afternoon' use.

I, too, make a point of recognising that rooms have a particular function at a particular time of day. I design houses so that you will be in the rooms when the sun is in them and furnish them to fit their function. Accordingly, your rooms need to be positioned, at the initial design stage, to receive sunlight at the times when you will be using them.

The starting point to getting this right is, once again, the site. By tracking the movements of the sun, you can begin to plot where, on the site, different functions of your home might be best located. Take note of where the sun rises, and sets, and how far the light penetrates in summer and winter. Consider shadows cast by trees and buildings. Plan to place unexciting service rooms in shaded areas of the site, leaving sunny areas for kitchens and living spaces.

orientation and solar gain are key aspects of sunny homes and eco-design.

Orientation considers the location of your house and the direction it faces. Orientation determines how little, or how much, sunlight your house will receive.

In northern latitudes of around 54°N–55°N (such as Belfast, Edinburgh, Copenhagen and Moscow), there are potentially 17 hours of sunlight in the summer, compared with only seven-and-a-half hours in the winter. Only south-facing surfaces have the potential to receive sunlight all year round. Surfaces orientated to the south-east, or south-west, will receive around ten per cent less sun than those facing south, whilst north-facing surfaces will be in shade all year round. The strength of the sun depends on its height above the horizon. In these northern latitudes, the sun in December at 12 noon barely scrapes 12 degrees above the horizon. This is the same height, and therefore the same strength, as the sun in June at 8.00am!

The sun's contribution to the internal heat of your home is called 'solar gain'. Maximising solar gain is central to creating an energy-efficient and light-efficient home. So concentrate full-height, vertical glazing on walls facing between south-east and south-west.

plan your home so that you will be using the rooms when the sun is in them

I love visiting a site for the first time. I always try to find the spot where I most enjoy standing.

This may be the place that gives me the best views of the site, or where I can feel a little sun. Then, I imagine which room of the house I would like to be in, at that moment. My aim is to position the principal rooms of the house (i.e. living room, family room and kitchen) to track the sun, whilst taking advantage of the best views.

kitchens should enjoy the sunlight from early morning to late evening because you are going to be there at all times of the day. This isn't as difficult as it might sound. The rising sun could come in through a high-level, gable window, casting warmth across the ceiling. The midday sun could enter through a glazed roof, giving heat and sunlight whilst you are enjoying your lunch. In the evening, the setting sun could warm your dining area through a western, glass wall.

living rooms and family rooms are mostly occupied during the afternoon and the evening. Accordingly, these rooms benefit from a southerly and, ideally, a westerly aspect.

find the best place on the site, then imagine which room you would like to be in at that moment

bedrooms are more about the views than the sunlight. I always ensure that the main bedroom enjoys the best view. Children's bedrooms are not so crucial (and having experience of teenagers who never raise their blinds, I am not sure they should have windows at all!).

dining spaces can be designed to reflect the mood of the space, perhaps by using sunlight to create a feeling of warmth, or by using shade to create a more romantic setting. So, don't worry about dining spaces: instead, prioritise the core living and kitchen areas.

utility spaces need lots of storage and so need fewer windows and more wall space. They are therefore useful spaces to plan into north-facing parts of the site. The same is true of bathrooms and toilets, which require a degree of privacy.

No-one has the perfect site. But there is no reason why you cannot create perfection by having an open mind. For example, north-facing sites, with north-facing views, can still enjoy sunny terraces. You can adopt a single-storey design that allows the sun to pass over the house, onto the terrace. You can also compensate for heat lost through north-facing glazing by using areas of south-facing glass in the roofs. This glass will fill the rooms beneath with sunlight and maximise solar gain.

cherish your trees

Mature trees provide an instant setting for your new home.

Planning officials recognise this, which is why tree surveys have to be carried out and you have to show that mature trees will not suffer as a result of your proposals. Some trees carry a Tree Preservation Order (TPO): these trees must not be lopped, topped or removed without approval from the Planning authority.

Considering mature trees at the design stage – which means actually designing your house around the trees – pays dividends with Planners. It also gives you an established setting that would otherwise take a long time to create.

For many years, I've used digital surveyors, who plot all the site's trees, contours, rocks and waterways on to a drawing. This becomes the template for all design work. When I worked as a young graduate in Princeton, New Jersey, my colleague, Leyla – a large, plain-speaking, Honduran woman – would thump a standard window catalogue on top of my precious drawings and drawl: "Time to get some reality into this, honey!" I soon learned that it's best to know where your boundaries are as early on in the design process as possible. The digital survey is my 'virtual Leyla': I can't fantasise that an idea will work if, in reality, it won't.

So, when you are designing your house:

- Keep the perimeter of the house, and its associated drainage, outside the canopy of mature trees. This means you will avoid damaging tree roots, because the canopy approximates to the root spread.

- Avoid lowering the ground around mature trees. This will lower the water table, on which the roots depend, and you risk killing the tree.

- Protect the roots of mature trees from heavy traffic. Do this by fencing off work on the site.

- Augment existing mature trees with new, additional, tree planting.

- Plant open areas of field as 'wildlife corridors' and woodland walks.

- Engage a landscape specialist early in the design process. They can sharpen your vision and give technical advice on your choice of indigenous trees and plants.

- Include the landscape drawing with your Planning submission. Any landscaping that is integral to the Planning approval for a new dwelling may be zero-rated for UK VAT, if it is completed at the same time as the house.

don't waste waterways

Natural waterways can be a wonderful bonus to any site, whether they be gushing mountain streams or fern-laced dams.

Even a sheugh or a boggy area can be developed, subject to permission from the relevant authority, into a natural wildlife area and enhance the setting of your house.

When I created the Origami House, I took care to design it around a hundred-year-old dam. This dam was originally built to power a water-wheel that ran a corn grinder, across the fields on my old farm. All the fallen trees were removed from the dam, the rotten sluice-gate was replaced and the stonework repaired. I carefully researched the flooding history of the site, measured the water-levels along the water-course and set the level of the house accordingly. The very weekend we moved into our new home witnessed the worst flooding in Northern Ireland for over a century. A very anxious night was spent watching the flood-water rage over the dam, and without even a sandbag for comfort! The noise was incredible. Next morning, the water level had fallen back to a gentle flow, and the dam had not been breached, although all my new plants that had been lining its banks were now a long way downstream!

So if you can hold your nerve, here are some thoughts on how to make the most of waterways:

Mountain streams, or even small ditches, can be used to separate public arrival areas from private areas around the house. An elegant bridge, or a broad-raised terrace, can be built to cross the waterway. The act of leaving the car behind, and crossing a bridge to reach the house, will highlight the contrast between the place of arrival, and the privacy of your home.

Old dams, or ponds made from natural bog, offer the prospect of a unique, water-filled setting for your home. With existing dams, first ensure there is no flooding history and that all sluice gates and outflows are in full working order. Then, plan part of your building to wrap around the water, using floor-to-ceiling glazing to embrace the watery scene. If you can choreograph the approach to your house from across the waterway, you will get fabulous reflections of your house in the water throughout the day.

even small streams can be used to enhance the setting of your house

frame beautiful views

It's the easiest thing in the world to put a big window in a wall and think you've captured the view.

However, to really capture it you need to choreograph the view as you want to see it from the room. This means choosing the best angle and then framing the view, as you would a picture. So if you have a great view, there's a lot more to think about than simply putting up acres of glass.

Firstly, position the priority spaces on the site (living, kitchen and main bedroom) where they can enjoy the best views. If the good views are northerly, compensate for heat lost through north-facing windows by using south-facing areas of glass roof for solar gain. For two-storey houses with north-facing views, locate living and entertaining areas on the first floor so that, again, areas of glass roof can be used to compensate for the heat lost through north-facing windows. As a general guide, balance out heat loss with solar gain by framing northerly views with smaller windows that are contained within the wall, and southerly views with larger window-wall glazing.

Secondly, position all the wet areas (utility rooms, bathrooms and en suites) and circulation spaces (staircases and corridors) towards areas of the site where the views are not so good, and where you can live with small windows or, indeed, none at all.

As I've said already, no-one has the perfect site. Invariably there are all sorts of blots on the landscape; someone else's unattractive house, electricity pylons or an unkempt agricultural shed. Framing beautiful views, whilst screening out poorer ones, is an additional challenge.

Rather than trying to screen these unfortunate views with landscaping, which will take a long time to mature, a better strategy is to deal with them at the design stage and use the form of the house, and its layout, to do most of the work for you.

I have designed a number of houses on sites that are adjacent to busy roads, but none more challenging than the Bawn House (opposite), in Ulster. This site was along a main dual carriageway and, because it was a replacement dwelling, we could not build anywhere else. The clients were faced with a wall of noise, dirt and visual intrusion. It was time for me to deploy my arsenal of contemporary design secrets:

- the first line of defence was to build a landscaped mound along the roadside, planted with dense trees and shrubbery, to both reflect and absorb road noise.
- the second was to use the shape of the building to buffer the road noise, creating a tranquil courtyard on the other side of the house.
- the third was to extend the walls of the house into the garden to create screen walls, which blocked views of the road. At the same time, they created privacy and framed the view of the garden as seen from the house.

for roadside sites, deploy the full arsenal of contemporary design secrets to create privacy and frame the view

embracing the landscape

Up until the seventeenth century, English stately homes were intentionally positioned in the landscape with a view to dominating it and projecting the owner's sense of superiority and authority.

regardless of size let your house embrace the landscape, and the design of your house respond to it

The great British architect Sir John Vanburgh changed all that. His design for Castle Howard, one of Yorkshire's finest stately homes and which was completed in 1712, turned conventional wisdom on its head.

Vanburgh's innovation was to approach the house from the side, rather than from the front. This allowed the grand frontage of the house to enjoy the view, rather than be the view. It was a revolutionary change in perspective – literally. For Vanburgh, the landscape was not something to be overcome but something that could choreograph views of the house from the countryside. This became the new model for stately homes – and there is no better example of this than Powerscourt, Dublin (opposite).

You might not be building a stately home but the idea of embracing the landscape, and allowing your house to respond to it, is fundamental to good rural design.

choreograph your approach

When approaching a house, we mentally prepare ourselves to see it and experience the spaces within.

There are three main types of approach: frontal, oblique and spiral. Each can be compressed into either a short distance, or expanded over hundreds of metres, depending on the size of your site.

Choosing the right version for my clients means getting to know them first! Together, we settle on an entrance sequence that best reflects their personalities, what they feel most comfortable with, and how they wish to receive their guests.

the approach to your house should reflect your personality, and how you wish to receive guests

Frontal approaches. These lead directly to the entrance in a straight, and usually axial, path. The secret here is ensuring that what you terminate your view with must be in proportion to the expectations you have set up in your approach. If the approach is very long, you need to terminate the view with the entire front façade of the house, or an elaborate entranceway within the front façade, because this gives grandeur and a sense of occasion upon arrival. The frontal approach is the architectural equivalent of a trumpet fanfare. For that reason, it is best reserved for those blessed with supreme confidence, or those who live a very public life, even in private.

Oblique approaches. These allow you to see several sides of the building at once. They help show off the form of the building and enhance the perspective of the different façades. By 'turning' the oblique approach, in a zig-zag across the site, you can display several aspects of the house as you approach. I find this works best with buildings that have a complex shape.

Spiral approaches. These extend the entrance sequence around the house. This allows you to glimpse the building from different angles, through framed views, perhaps using landscaping as screens. Sometimes the building is simply hidden, until it is revealed at the entrance. This principle works equally well whether in a carefully planned small garden or a vast estate.

Oblique and spiralling approaches are best suited to those with a more carefree outlook, or an instinctive curiosity for life.

create spaces around your house

When I start with a bare site, I aim to leave the site with the feeling it is bigger with the building on it than it was without the building.

The secret here is in forming the building in such a way that it creates a variety of spaces around it.

And, just like the spaces you create within your home, the spaces you create around your home can be used for different purposes. We need to maximise the potential of space around the house as much as we do for space within the house. Think of these outdoor spaces as 'rooms' and think about their function. It is important to consider this at the outset so you can get them in the right places, even though they will be designed in detail later.

All you need to do at this stage is 'zone' these spaces into public, semi-public and private spaces.

Public spaces are accessible by everyone, not least the arrival area for visitors, postmen and even unwanted callers! This can be either a formal forecourt, or simply a parking and turning area within the landscape.

shape your building to create spaces around it – these spaces are as important as the building itself

Semi-private spaces are areas which you might think of as private but which can be overlooked by visitors. For example, in the house opposite, the small landscaped recess between two stone pavilions forms a small semi-private, courtyard. This gives access from the main parking area to the back door, which is hidden from public view by the deep stone wall.

Private spaces are areas to which only you have access; for example, a sunny terrace, outside dining area or enclosed garden.

When zoning your outside spaces, make sure that:

- the arrival space for visitors connects to the front door from the driveway.
- semi-private spaces (like an inner courtyard) are positioned beyond the arrival area.
- private spaces are concealed (e.g. by garden walls, landscaping, or even the shape of the house).

plan for the car

When designing a home in the country, it's only natural for people to think first about the house!

However, cars are a necessity if you live in the country and their practical demands are great (e.g. parking, turning and garaging). So you need to take account of this at the outset, otherwise you run the risk of compromising your design later on.

In my experience, clients' attitudes to the car and its importance vary wildly. One young couple nearly came to blows when, halfway through the build, the well-meaning, car-loving husband wanted to change the parking arrangements. Instead of the discreet rear courtyard we had planned, he now wanted a large, hotel-style, roundabout at the front of the house. This meant that my elegantly-designed front veranda was now destined to overlook a car park. So I was more than a little intrigued when his wife took me aside and asked me to leave the issue with her. A few months later – with no further mention of the offending roundabout – I decided to raise the thorny issue, only to be told we were reverting to the original layout. I looked to her husband for confirmation of this change of heart but he just smiled. I nearly fell off the scaffolding when she said, in front of the brickies, that she had refused to make love to him until he agreed!

By contrast, and all too often, rural houses are simply surrounded by a sea of tarmac. Although this seems to solve all access problems, it totally destroys your privacy and you end up having awkward conversations with the postman whilst you are sunbathing.

By giving some thought to the car before you start on-site, you can guard your privacy – and halve your tarmacing bill. So remember:

- visitors' cars belong firmly in the public space and should not encroach on private spaces around the house.
- your own car should move through this public space to a semi-private area, such as a carport or rear courtyard.
- people will park their cars as close to the front door as humanly possible. So you should plan broad paths and planting areas between the parking and the house to screen parked cars. This ensures that rooms facing these areas will always have an attractive outlook.

> plan broad paths and planting areas between the house and the courtyard to screen parked cars and give an attractive outlook

create enclosure on arrival

Even before you enter a house, some public arrival spaces make you feel welcome whilst others leave you feeling distinctly uncomfortable. This is because buildings are a bit like people.

We respond to buildings in a similar way to how we respond to people. St. Peter's Basilica in Rome is a case in point. When the Italian architect Gian Lorenzo Bernini designed the forecourt to the Basilica, he cleverly balanced the rather imposing Renaissance façade of the Basilica with two magnificent colonnades that extended outwards, like arms, as if embracing the people. Bernini understood that how you design a building helps to shape emotional responses.

create an intimacy upon arrival by reducing the scale of the building's form and detail

One secret to creating a welcoming building is to design 'enclosure'. The key elements of enclosure are: form, scale, and character.

form. If the building is large enough, you can create enclosure using the shape of the building itself (like Bernini's colonnades). In the case of smaller buildings, enclosure can be achieved by using garages, barns and garden walls. Even landscaping, too, can form enclosure. Siting a house near existing trees or mature hedges gives instant definition to at least two sides of the public space, with the house and the garage forming the other two sides.

scale. Scale is a product of height and size. You have to balance the height of the buildings which surround the enclosure with the size of the public space. Because this is your home – and not a municipal headquarters – you want to create intimacy. So:

- For a single-storey house, the enclosure should be approximately 10m across.
- For a two-storey house, the enclosure should be approximately 15m across.
- Use over-arching tree canopies to give the illusion of a ceiling. This will reduce the scale of the public space.
- Keep boundary walls and hedges about 1.5m high. This will be enough to give shelter and privacy without being intimidating.

character. The character of the enclosure should reflect the character of the building. To create a welcoming mood, you need to bring sunlight into the public space. Keep two-storey buildings to the north, where they won't cast a shadow. Create a calming effect, by using the sound of running water (e.g. a natural water feature, or a contemporary fountain). You can also use soft landscaping (e.g. the rustle of bamboos) or the aroma of herb gardens and lavender-lined walls.

make your house the right height

The height of your home is not something to boast about at work, nor is it a good indication of how successful you were with the Planners! Like everything else, the number of storeys should reflect what suits the site – and what suits you.

Some people have a real hang-up about the height of their house. Once I advised a client that if he wanted to move his Planning-approved, two-storey house design from a hollow to a hilltop, he would have to change the design to a single-storey. He turned to his wife, and sighed: "Darling, we're getting a bungalow." I hadn't realised until that point the depth of people's negative feelings about bungalows. I grew up in one – and loved it! So it was a surprise to me how much some people hated the idea of living in a bungalow. But having worked as an architect in Northern Ireland for 20 years, and having seen the proliferation of what I call 'Georgianesque bungalows' (which are basically rectangular boxes with Georgian windows), I can understand why some people may feel short-changed.

It was in response to this client's comment that I decided I wanted to design 'the new rural bungalow'. Clearly, there was a challenge. Sometimes, the best solution for a site in the country is a single-storey design, for many different reasons, one of which is the need to reduce visual impact. But the proliferation of 'Georgianesque bungalows' isn't down to the Planners who, in my experience, are always keen to embrace diversity. The real problem has been its ease of repetition: having been approved in the past, the 'Georgianesque bungalow' is still the quickest route to gaining Planning approval.

I wanted my clients to see there was a better way of designing single-storey houses, and for people to see them as exciting homes to live in. Over the last decade, I have explored the idea of single-storey living in the landscape, through a series of ground-breaking pavilion houses, which are featured in this book.

Single-storey houses have certain advantages. They can be fully accessible for the disabled or infirm and are ideal 'lifetime homes'. They can boast sculpted ceilings throughout, giving ground floor rooms a luxurious sense of space. It's true that two-storey dwellings have advantages over single-storeys. You can create double-height spaces; and bedrooms, when located upstairs, are more secure. However, two-storey dwellings also have disadvantages. Ground floor rooms will nearly all have flat ceilings, and this can be monotonous. The one-and-a-half-storey house, unfortunately, tends to be a compromise: it can neither achieve the grandeur of the two-storey, nor can it offer the sculptural space of the single-storey.

I wanted to design 'the new rural bungalow' – one that would be uplifting to look at and exciting to live in

make your building belong to its setting

Integrating your house with the landscape doesn't mean making it invisible. The important thing is that it belongs to its setting. It can do this in many ways, sometimes by being similar to other features in the landscape, at other times, by daring to be different.

When choosing the position for your house, you could just make life easy for yourself, from a Planning point of view, and build where the house will be hidden from view, even if it means building in a hole, on a north-facing site. But that is hardly going to be a home worth investing in, never mind somewhere you will enjoy living. So whilst you need to understand the Planners' perspective, you may also have to challenge their boundaries and be prepared to argue for what you think will be the best result.

As you do so, be aware that Planning assessments are not judged simply against a rigid checklist. Instead, your design will be assessed, on its merits, against the broader issues of integration with the setting, its scale and massing, and therefore its height, and its materials – all, again, in response to the local context.

whilst you are still designing your building, appreciate how the Planners are likely to view your proposals

So, Planners will consider the character of what has been built in the local area, and prefer if your house was similar in scale and, sometimes, character (particularly, if it is a conservation area). If your proposed house is in the context of small cottages it might seem, at first, that you have no option but to apply for something similar. However, if your particular site has a different context, such as on a hill, overlooking a valley of riverside cottages, then it could be argued with the Planners that your house should respond differently to this unique setting. So you shouldn't feel that you have to give up at the first hurdle, nor produce a design that appeals to the 'lowest Planning denominator'. You could argue, instead, that a hillside house is designed to hold the expansive view of the valley, like a traditional landlord's house, and, as a reciprocal response, it becomes part of that view. The point here is that, even though your design is strikingly different, it is nevertheless in response to the setting. In particular, it has a historical reference point. By contrast, the riverside cottages were probably built as labourers' cottages and their size and relationship to the river for water was a necessity of that time. The point is that the same landscape can produce very different buildings, and still be the product of a particular, historical, reference point.

cope with slopes

Sloping sites tend to put clients off, with fears of a costly house sliding down the hill! But flattening the site and 'helicoptering' in a standardised house will inevitably look contrived, because the setting was artificially constructed to begin with.

I love designing on sloping sites. Aside from the challenge, they are part of a wider, sloping landscape and make wonderful settings because of the views beyond the house.

where possible, aim to enter the house from above and then to move down through its interior spaces

Some valley sites level off at the bottom and, although it can be tempting to build on this flat part, the result can feel oppressive, as if the weight of the surrounding land is crowding in on you. It is like living in a quarry. Instead, work with the grain of the ground, like the Lough Beg House opposite. Keep the house up on the slope and step the building down the hillside, with small changes of level. The result is that your perspective of the landscape will change as you move down through the house – giving you four views, not just one!

So try to remember that:

- **if approaching from below**, tall buildings will look taller and the proportions of vertical elements (such as narrow windows and tall chimneys) will be exaggerated. To allow for this visual distortion, I suggest playing down the overall height of the building (i.e. its ridge height), and to counterbalance vertical features with strong, horizontal, elements such as balconies, guttering and long, horizontal, panes of glass.

- **if approaching from above**, your perspective is foreshortened and the building has an unfortunate tendency to look squat. To counterbalance this effect, vertical elements should, this time, be exaggerated. This means stretching chimneys, and emphasising windows with vertical mullions and tall panes of glass, like the Lough Beg House, opposite.

the look of the house

This is inevitably going to be a product of your personal journey and inspirations. I can see this process reflected in the finished look of my own Origami House.

I was raised (or 'rared' as they say in County Antrim) in a beautiful 1960s flat-roofed bungalow. Looking back, many of the features I loved about it have subconsciously influenced the look of my own house. I appreciated its open-plan, floor-to-ceiling windows and outside terrace, as well as its integration of inside and outside living spaces. And, having grown up in the countryside, I wanted to build a house there – and to do so with a strong sense of rural responsibility.

your house design should lift your heart every time you come home

Later, when I studied Architecture at the Universities of Manchester and Bath, I was stirred by Manchester's extravagant Victorian chimneys and by Bath's timeless Georgian architecture. These inspirations, too are reflected in my own tall chimneys and the human scale of my pavilioned Origami House.

Yet another influence was my time as Rome Scholar at the British School in Rome. Whether Ferragamo shoes or Ferrari cars, the Italians do everything with style! So I, too, wanted my house to be beautiful – somewhere that would lift my heart.

Just like me, you will find that your own inspirations will affect the look of your house including its roof, chimneys, walls and windows.

the roof

The roof is the most important element in the design of your house. Whether flat or pitched, metal or slate, it sets the overall tone and character.

However, the roof is not only important from an aesthetic point of view, it is probably also the most expensive. Your choice of materials for the roof will also have far-reaching consequences for the design, and construction, of everything below it.

if your house is going to be approached from above, a beautiful roof is crucial

You might think that, with so many different roofing materials to choose from (including natural slate, composite tiles, sheet metal or thatch) that the choice is endless and, in a sense, it is. However, you do need to make your choice at the outset and budget for it accordingly. Very often you will not be able to change the roofing materials when on-site because too many constructional decisions have already been made which are possible with one material, but not with another. For example, structural calculations for the roof reflect the weight of the material on it. This material then determines the roof's pitch and its detailing at ridges, verges and valleys.

The choice of fibre cement slates, or concrete tiles – which are quite thick – place major constraints on your design. These products will necessarily result in clunky and heavy-handed detailing because that is what they lend themselves to. If you want a Ferrari roof, you have to use Ferrari products. For this reason, my personal favourites for designing roofs in the countryside are natural slate and metal, which lend themselves to a sharp, contemporary look.

natural slate roofs

I have used natural slate on pitched roofs for over 20 years. I love the idea of taking something natural straight out of the ground, and putting it on the roof. It's as if the ground becomes our umbrella.

Clients today have an enormous choice in slate:

- the Penrhyn or 'Bangor Blue' Welsh slate is regarded as the best quality slate in the world. It is still hand-finished by skilled workers in Welsh slate mines – see over. The heather, blue/purple colour has a warmth that rival slates find hard to match. Due to the consistency of the slate in both thickness and flatness, it lays beautifully, giving a uniform surface and an excellent weathering resistance.

Penrhyn slate quarry, Bethesda, Wales

- Spanish slate is a very good alternative and a more economical choice as Spain now has 75% of the world's production of slate.

- Over the last 15 years, China has emerged as another player in the slate market as has, even more recently, Brazil. Both provide competitive options but durability varies wildly. Durablity depends on the structure of the slate and the absence of deleterious minerals that break down on exposure to the elements. Slates with high carbonate or metal sulphide levels should be avoided.

One of the great advantages of natural slate is that roof valleys, hips and verges can all be specially designed to enhance the clean lines of your house. A slim slate, ideally around 6mm thick, with a smooth, but not-too-riven surface, will lend a precise look to your roof.

metal roofs

whilst traditional thatched roofs need to be replaced every 15 years, a copper or zinc roof will last over one hundred years

Metal roofs go back to Roman times, when copper was first used as a roofing material. Despite their antiquity, metal roofs seem to us very modern. As well as copper, other materials make attractive roofs, including zinc, aluminium and stainless steel. Although metal roofs are expensive, they have lots of advantages:

- **sustainability** – Although metals are non-renewable resources, they are all completely recyclable.

- **longevity** – Metal roofs offer minimal maintenance and can last for one hundred years (unlike a thatch roof).

- **versatility** – Unlike slate roofs, metal roofs can be used on roofs with a low pitch (i.e. lower than 30 degrees).

- **speed of installation** – Metal roofs can be put on in a day. They are laid in sheets and zipped together on-site to create a standing seam that is waterproof, yet allows for thermal movement of the metal. These seams create visually strong lines running from ridge to gutter, which gives the metal roof its contemporary look.

- **weight** – Metal roofs are lightweight and so the underlying supporting structure can be lighter, which may result in lower costs.

If you are going to have a metal roof make sure that, when mixing your metals, you avoid direct contact between incompatible materials. Be careful not to put, for example, galvanised roofing and stainless steel downpipes together, because this can cause galvanic corrosion. This occurs when one material corrodes onto the other material, because of its place on the Galvanic Corrosion Table – a wonderful table that ranks metals according to their 'nobility'. The less noble metals in the table, such as zinc and aluminium, are more likely to be attacked by the noble ones, such as gold and graphite. The greater the difference between the two joined metals, depending on where they are on the table, the greater potential there is for galvanic corrosion. So, do be aware of the consequences of mixing metals when designing your roof, valleys, roof verges and guttering.

glass in the roof

As well as the actual covering of your roof, you can also think about how to use the roof to bring light into the building.

You can do this either by using standard roof windows, or bespoke areas of glass in the roof. This is often a smart move because the same area of glass is three times more effective at bringing light into a room when placed on a roof than a window in a wall. This is because glass on the roof is inclined towards the sky. The further up the roof the glass is positioned, the greater the penetration of light.

Glass in the roof is very useful for bringing warm sunlight into buildings on difficult sites that might not otherwise have it. This includes sites with north-facing views, or where the south-facing views are either poor, or lack privacy. I use huge roof lights, sometimes six metres in length. From below, they don't look like windows. You don't see the framing, only the rafters. It is as if the slates have simply been peeled back to reveal the sky.

Glass in the roof is particularly important in latitudes greater than 55°N, such as in Ireland and Scotland, because we have so few hours of daylight in winter and most of these are spent working, or living, indoors. This can lead to Seasonal Affective Disorder (SAD), whose symptoms include depression, low energy, oversleeping, and overeating. Therefore, we need to find ways of bringing in as much natural daylight and sunlight as possible.

Glass in the roof should suit the design of the building. The framing needs to be aluminium, rather than timber, to make it maintenance-free. For the same reason, roof glazing should always be fitted with self-cleaning glass. Instead of looking like boxes set onto the roof, roof glazing can be designed to be sleek and sit level with the slates. It can be formed into an apex on the roof to make a double roof light. It can even be shaped like a contemporary lantern to light a special living or dining space.

use south-facing roof lights in rooms with north-facing views to flood the space with sunlight and balance out any heat lost through north-facing windows

the chimneys

Unlike roofs and walls, chimneys do not have to be a key feature of the look of your house. However, they can bring a touch of exuberance to a building.

From the Gothic period onwards, chimneys were a key part of the architectural skyline. Some were disproportionately tall and extravagantly decorated with ornamental stonework; others rose from the ground like giant buttresses.

Elaborate chimneys were not restricted to large stately homes but were repeated, particularly in the Victorian period, on smaller, single-storey, gate lodges. Decorative chimneys could also be found in manor houses and larger farmhouses at the turn of the twentieth-century. You can still tour the countryside and spot the signature brickwork of particular chimney-builders. So the chimney as a key feature of houses in the countryside has a rich architectural history. Their height, in contrast to the building, adds drama to it whilst their shape provides endless opportunities for light and shade.

However, despite all these historical reference points, Planners tend to have great difficulty with chimneys as a design feature. There is a sense in which the model for rural design remains the little cottage in which the chimney is simply embedded in the gable of the wall and is not expressed as a design feature. For this reason, Planners operate strict rules about chimneys on rural dwellings. This means that chimneys should be located on the apex of the roof, because that is where they were traditionally placed on small cottages. Planners also prefer chimneys to be kept low, just about a metre above the apex of the roof. They also like them to be built off the gable of the wall, rather than expressed as a buttress.

At the same time, design guides are only that: guides. Planners look at each case on its own merits. So you should be able to make a case for the chimney that you want. If you want to use the chimney as a key design feature, make sure your chimney is firmly embedded in your design and, as such, is a response to the setting.

I love chimneys – for me, they are sculptures in the sky

the walls

External walls are another important element in defining the look of your rural house.

This is because, historically, the first major structures built in the countryside were Stone Age forts ('raths'), and Norman castles. Visually, these were solid masses of stone, with few openings, because their primary role was for enclosure and defence. The next wave of rural buildings was stone cottages. These cottages were, in the main, built from unhewn field stone, so openings were hard to form and were therefore small.

The widespread introduction of glass in the mid 17th-century could have meant more windows; however, the introduction of the 'Window Tax' in 1696 (which was really a tax on houses scaled according to the number of windows) curtailed the general use of windows for all but the wealthy. This ensured the dominance of the wall over the openings within it. By the time the Window Tax was repealed in 1851, the supremacy of wall over window was firmly established.

your contemporary rural house can enjoy the benefits of lots of glass and, at the same time, respect the traditional form of rural buildings

This is why Planning authorities nowadays talk about a high 'wall to window' ratio as a criterion for building in the countryside. It is also the reason why the typical '1970s' bungalow with its large picture-windows looks incongruous in the rural setting – it is not consistent with our rural architectural heritage. The Planners' response to the 1970s bungalow was to insist on smaller windows, which resulted in the 'Georgianesque bungalow' we see today. The latter was then 'rubber-stamped' across the countryside, without regard to the demands of form and setting we explored earlier.

As a result, people's perception of Planning today is that you cannot have a lot of glass in your rural house. But this isn't true. After all, my work – which features lots of glass! – is based in greenbelt areas throughout the countryside, which are difficult to build in, as far as Planning is concerned. Yet all the houses I design meet strict Planning guidelines for these areas.

The secret to using glass in contemporary rural design is to concentrate areas of glass into single large panes, so that the visual emphasis remains on the mass of the wall. This ensures that the building will be perceived as weighty, and anchored to the land, even though, in places, the building is conjoined with nature through glass. Another way of emphasising this sense of weight is by putting a very small window into a large mass of wall. This will make the wall appear even weightier in contrast to the small scale of the window within it.

white masonry walls

The white-masonry house in the countryside has a strong tradition.

When the Normans conquered Leinster in 1169, they built a whitewashed castle on a hill. This could be seen from afar, establishing their authority and occupation beyond question. It was the most 'in-your-face' architectural statement they could make: just as well they didn't need Planning permission! It was not until the eighteenth century that rural cottages began to be constructed in the countryside. People used whatever rough-hewn stones were lying around and, with only hand tools available, the stone was hard to work and results were crude. Because of the ragged outline of the stonework, doors and windows were hard to weatherproof. Render was ultimately introduced to cover up the stonework and sometimes to provide better weather proofing. These rendered walls were then either lime-washed or painted white.

Today there are lots of modern self-coloured and textured renders to choose from, however, some can be problematic in our temperate climate. Personally, I prefer using a traditional sand-cement render, either rough-dash or smooth. Rough-dash render using a fine, pit gravel, or smooth render, using a fibre in both the scratch and float coats, are excellent finishes for the contemporary house. Painting the sand-cement render every five years with a good-quality breathable paint will freshen it like new every time.

White walls contrast visually with the green landscape. They also contrast with glass, which looks dark in daytime. This lends a black-and-white sculptured look to the building. The white walls accentuate the solids of the building, while the glass accentuates the voids. This creates a different aesthetic to a stone building, because the combination of dark stone and dark glass means you are only able to accentuate solids and voids at night, when there is a contrast between the darkness of the stone walls and the illuminated interiors.

personally, my two favourite wall types are white masonry and stone – these are the materials most rooted in the heritage of our landscape

stone walls

Like white walls, stone walls have always been a strong feature of the rural scene, be they in stone cottages, or in fields defining their patterns. Stone is thus a key aesthetic of the countryside. However, as with any aesthetic, it has to be handled carefully.

Stone is a particularly difficult material to use. Because of its colour and texture, stone can very quickly overpower your design. Unless the form of the house is very clear, for example, if it is circular, the beauty of the form of the house will be smothered by the visual complexity of the stone. However, simply cladding the front façade of the house in stone, leaving the rest rendered, is not the answer either – it will just look as though you couldn't afford to finish the job. So, even though stone provides a fabulous finish, it usually benefits from a light touch. To be successful with stone, it needs to be part of the design from the outset and budgeted accordingly. As with roofs, it is not usually possible to change your mind about the materials at a later stage.

The Lough View House (opposite) is sheltered within the embrace of a mighty curved stone retaining wall that holds back the landscape. I used massive stone chimneys to contrast with the overall white masonry wall and glass aesthetic of this house. It is an example of how contrasting the use of stone with other materials makes it more affordable and helps to emphasise the key design idea.

You need good quality stone-masonry to achieve a beautiful stone wall. Stone, and in particular un-hewn field stone, needs to be skilfully laid in horizontal courses. Otherwise you run the risk of it looking like Tinkerbell's castle in Disneyland, where the walls aren't stone at all but are really concrete panels (I hope I haven't shattered any illusions!). Here are some secrets to successful building with stone:

- build the stone in horizontal courses 450mm deep.
- always use a lime mortar which is made with a very coarse sand.
- pointing should be either recessed, or semi-recessed.
- never use ribbon pointing to highlight the stonework – this is where the pointing protrudes beyond the face of the stone forming a ledge. This ledge catches rainwater and causes the stone to deteriorate in freezing conditions.

An increasingly popular stone, for the contemporary house, is slate. It is easily maintained, very durable and comes in a variety of colours, sizes and textures. It can be simply constructed as a load-bearing, cladding material. This can be tied back to the cavity wall, or fixed on metal fixings and frames for a thoroughly modern look.

stone benefits from a light touch: too much overpowers the design; too little looks as if you couldn't afford any more!

the windows

Around the turn of the sixteenth century, glazed windows were introduced as a rather luxurious item.

glass is the key element to connecting your living spaces to the landscape

Eleanor Godfrey, in her history of glass-making, notes how in 1590 an alderman in Doncaster left his house to his wife but the windows to his son – one can only imagine how that worked out! Similarly, the owners of Alnwick Castle always had their windows removed when they went away, just in case they were broken.

In contemporary houses today, glass is the key element to connecting your living space with the landscape and, with advances in technologies, heat loss is no longer the over-riding issue in its use.

placing windows in walls

Windows are important because their position and shape within the wall affects how light enters the room and the illumination of everything within:

- A window that is surrounded on all four sides by the wall (and does not, for example, go all the way down to the floor) will appear as a bright shape, compared to the rest of the shaded wall. This is why traditional, deep-set windows were flanked by splayed reveals, reducing glare and bouncing light further into the room. In modern houses, this is harder to achieve because modern walls are much less thick. However, you can alleviate glare by introducing a window on an adjacent wall, so daylight enters the room from at least two directions.

- A window positioned right in the corner of the wall will throw light along the adjacent internal wall. This means you don't get a dark area in the corner of the room.

- Two windows, together forming the corner of a room, help to give a more even distribution of light into the room. They are also better than two, separate, windows because, instead of making you look out of each window in turn, they lead your eye out of the corner of the window to appreciate a single, enhanced view.

Windows are also the crucial link between the interior space and the exterior landscape. Here, it helps to remember that:

- Small openings located wholly within the wall can frame a particular view. Large openings can take in a wider panoramic, serving either as the focus for a living area, or backdrop to a dining area.

- A series of windows within the wall can give snaps of the view as you move through the interior space. I tend to use these in active areas to enliven galleries and corridors.

window-walls make the space beyond the interior feel part of the room

Walls made entirely of glass (called 'window-walls') make you feel that the space beyond the interior is actually part of the room. This is because the vertical wall, which would otherwise enclose the space, has been replaced by glass. To create this fluid effect, you will of course be using a lot of glass. The problem here is that the larger your area of glass, the thicker the frames tend to be and this will impede the sense you are trying to create. So, aim to make your window frames as slim-line as possible. Window walls and windows that come right down to the floor have the added advantage that you can always enjoy the view whether sitting or standing.

The unseen advantage of the window-wall is the omission of the window sill. I used to live in an old farmhouse with deep window sills, which became dumping grounds for everything we should have thrown out, but didn't. When I moved to the Origami House, I wondered why it was much easier to keep tidy. I realised that it was because there wasn't a single window sill in the entire house!

window materials

Sustainability, maintenance and cost: these are the three key issues when considering window materials.

pvc:

This is an inexpensive, long-lasting and low maintenance option. PVC windows are available in white, colour and even wood effect but unfortunately still look like plastic and the material's environmental credentials are the lowest of all available window materials.

timber:

Hardwood, sourced from a managed forest, is an excellent option for windows if you can afford it. A stable hardwood makes a very good sliding door. Ayan, known in the building trade as 'poor man's oak', is a light-coloured hardwood that is a sustainable choice as well as being stable in an exterior environment. Unlike some other hardwoods, it also holds paint well. Western Red Cedar is a good choice if you want a natural colour. Heat can be lost even through solid timber, so use a frame which has a thermal break rather than a solid frame. This thermal break prevents direct heat loss through the solid material and is essential if you are going to the expense of triple glazing.

aluminium:

These window and door systems are the most expensive option. However, their powder-coated paint finish ensures they are maintenance-free and the range of colours is very extensive. When combined with thermally broken frames and thermal glazing they are especially good at minimising heat loss. Aluminium sliding door systems vary in the thickness of their frames – the slimmest being the most expensive.

As always, your choice of material needs to be in sympathy with your overall design. For example, aluminium window frames will be too harsh for a house that otherwise has a more natural aesthetic. On the other hand, they will be a fitting match for a precision-engineered look.

across the threshold

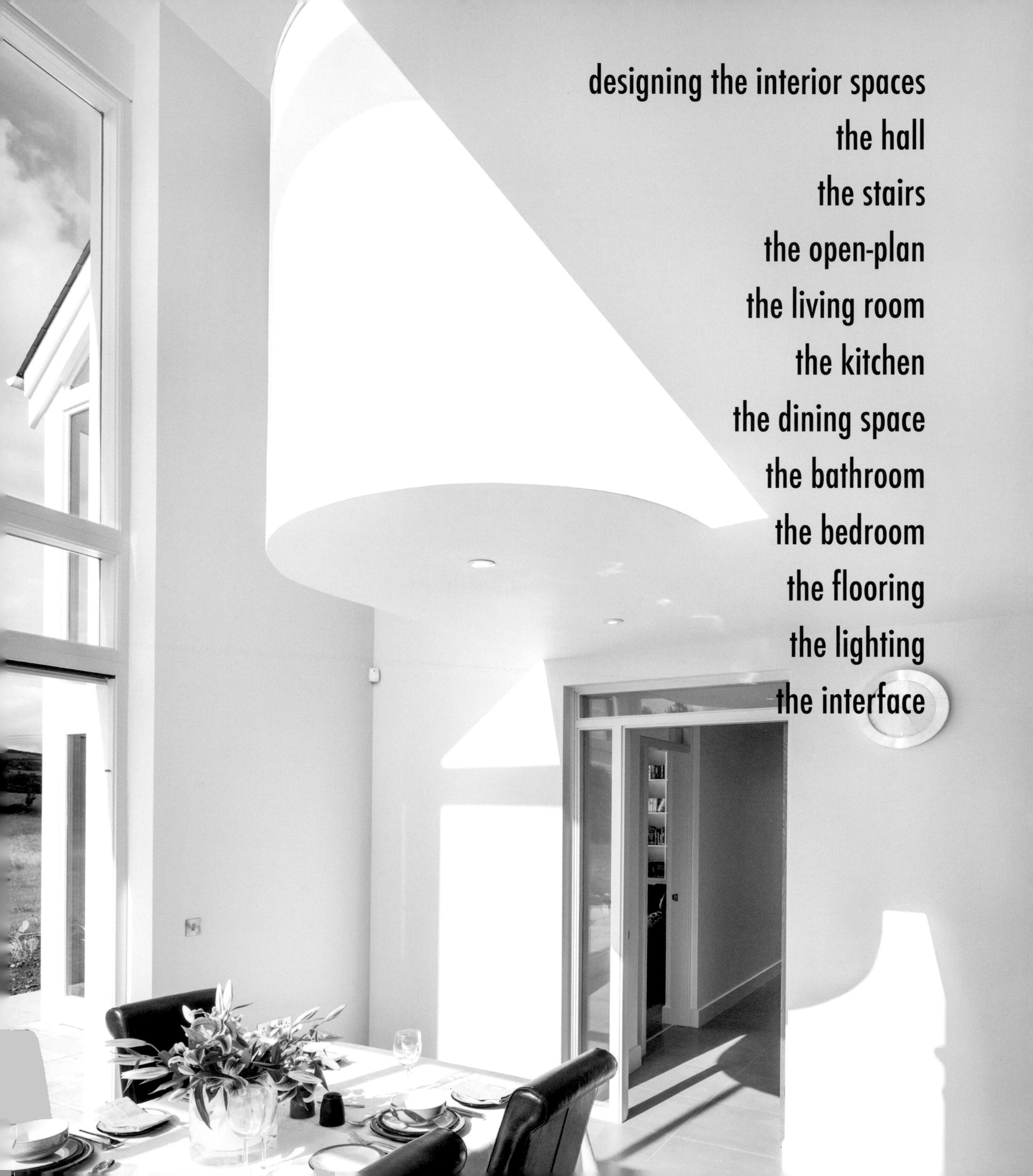

designing the interior spaces

the hall

the stairs

the open-plan

the living room

the kitchen

the dining space

the bathroom

the bedroom

the flooring

the lighting

the interface

designing the interior spaces

So far, we have explored the form of the building as set in the landscape.

think seriously about how the interior spaces are going to work for you

Once you have thought about all of that, you can then move across the threshold and focus more closely on the interior spaces. Now you can seriously think about how you are going to live in your new home and how each of the spaces are going to work for you.

Looking back at your mood board will give you a steer as to where on the overall spectrum you should locate your contemporary house. This will affect the design of your interior spaces including: the hall, the stairs, the open-plan, the living room, the kitchen, the dining space, the bathroom, the bedroom, and everywhere else.

The hall has a significant and unique role to play. It receives family and guests into the house. Some guests may never see further than your hall, so for them it is their only peep under the veil. The question for you therefore is: how much of the tone and character of your house do you want to reveal with the hall?

There are therefore two main ways of designing a hall:

- The hall can be an expression of the rest of your house. So you could have a big, impressive hall with long views looking up to a high gallery, or through to living and dining areas. The hall here is helping to give visitors a feeling of generosity. If it is going to be a big impressive hall then it is important that all the other spaces leading from the hall live up to the initial billing. Anything less will seem, to the visitor, like a crashing anticlimax.

- Alternatively, the hall can actually withhold the tone and character of the rest of your house, which then comes as a surprise. Your hall can be modest, just dealing with the functional requirements, giving carefully controlled, but intriguing glimpses of what lies beyond. This builds a sense of anticipation, which pays off as you progress through the house. The feeling may be one of moving through an exquisite Japanese garden, where the beauty is unveiled one step at a time and never all at once.

Just like the approach to your house, (which can be frontal, spiralling or oblique), the type of hall you go for is very much your personal choice. People whose lives are on public display may be attracted to the first option, while people who are a little more reserved may prefer the second.

If you have decided on a large hall, you still want to feel that you are entering a house and not a hotel. Large halls can be overwhelming. To mitigate this you could incorporate another function within the hall, such as a dining space. This will help furnish the hall and give it a homely aspect which you would not find in a hotel. If you have decided on a modest hall but still need some extra space (for example, because of pushchairs and wheelchairs) take the pressure off the hall by designing a large cloak-space, boot-room, or open-plan space within the hall, screened off by a partition wall, or twist of the staircase. This way you can take the extra functionality of storage and kit out of the hall and hide it round the corner. Your modest-sized hall gains the illusion of space because it only has to deal with receiving guests.

your hall might give carefully controlled glimpses of what lies beyond – as if you were moving through an exquisite Japanese garden

the stairs

The true drama queen will imagine themselves sweeping down a *Titanic*-style grand staircase, à la Kate Winslet. However, for most people, that moment is best captured at the Titanic Experience, Belfast, and not within your own home.

That's not to say contemporary staircases have to be boring either! Stair companies specialising in glass, steel and timber can make you just about anything nowadays. But you need to have the vision – and the space to put the vision in! There is no point in having a grand staircase if there is no room for it and you end up opening the front door only to walk into the bottom of the stairs. If you have decided on a big, impressive, hall, make sure you design it so that when you enter, you can stand far enough back to appreciate the staircase properly.

the statement stair If your stair is going to be a 'statement stair' – or focus of the hall – there are two main ways of doing this. You can cantilever the stairs off the walls of the hall, or the stairs can be free-standing and look like a piece of sculpture.

When I design statement stairs within the hall, I try to avoid arrangements where you are not able to look at your guests, as you greet them, the whole way down the stairs. It's a bit awkward saying 'hello' to your guests and then turning your back on them and then saying 'hello, again!'

bring stairs to life by bathing them in natural light

The statement stair should be wider than the typical domestic stair in order to lend it stature (around 1.3m to 1.5m is desirable). The hall should also be large enough to accommodate a graceful incline with a low rise and generous tread. In my view, stairs need natural light – and preferably sunlight – to bring them to life. Otherwise they can just feel like dead space. So try to locate your staircase where there are generous windows, or glass in the roof.

the secret stair If you have decided on a hall that is designed to create intrigue, the 'secret stair' will heighten the sense of anticipation. The 'hidden' or 'partially concealed' stair is positioned a little off the main route: they signify that you cannot ascend without an invitation. They evoke the spiral staircases within the turrets of Scottish baronial castles, and the cloistered alcoves of Renaissance courtyards. Whereas statement stairs deliver drama, secret stairs create suspense.

the open-plan

I was brought up in an open-plan house.

What I loved about this (notwithstanding the fact that telephone conversations with boyfriends tended to be brief!) was that sense of us as a family really living life together. Even though we might have been doing different things, we were aware of what each was doing which wouldn't have been the case if we had all been in separate rooms. I still visit the family home regularly and what I continue to admire about the open-plan is the way I feel instantly included in whatever is going on in the house at that moment.

My fascination for the open-plan was fuelled again when, as a young architect, I was asked to design and deliver a country retreat for the fifth-richest man in the world. I am still waiting for the call from the other four! At that time, I was fortunate enough to be working in the office of Michael Graves, one of the world's best-known architects, popularly known for the singing bird kettle which he designed for Alessi. From my American colleagues, whose national past-time was open-plan design, I learned that the key was to give every space within the open-plan its own function and character.

The ceiling, walls and floor can all be used to define the spaces within the open-plan.

the ceiling might seem an unlikely place to start but it is in fact a wonderful way of dividing up a room. In the house opposite, I designed the ceiling of the open-plan space with a dropped, flat ceiling to make the family living area cosy and raised the rest of the ceiling into a cathedral shape to give elegance to the dining area.

the internal walls define the spaces within the open-plan. They can separate a dining area within the living space or, with careful positioning, screen the prep area of the kitchen from view. Such walls can be straight, curved, solid or perforated and can be treated in different ways. I like to make the walls deep enough (about 300mm deep) so that they can take books, pictures, and sculptures; the wall itself therefore becomes another piece of personalised art.

the eye measures the size of the space by the longest diagonal it can see, so rooms with cathedral ceilings or glazed walls will appear bigger than their traditional equivalents

the external walls need not take the form of a big open rectangle. The walls can be shaped to create more interesting forms. Each of these external walls can themselves be fully-glazed, half-glazed or completely solid, depending on the function of each area. Kitchens will probably have solid walls because you will need to locate units on them, whereas living and dining rooms might look on to a view of the garden.

- **fully-glazed walls** I love connecting the inside of the house with the outside. Some might be worried, that with all this glass, they will feel like they are living in a field! This is undoubtedly a risk but you can avoid this by creating rooms with a sense of both space and intimacy. The traditional way of making a space feel 'cosy' was to create an inward-looking room (typically one with heavy walls, small windows and focussed on the fireplace). But contemporary houses are about creating outward-looking rooms that connect with the landscape. You can be contemporary and cosy by carefully designing the interior space, so that your ceiling height, lighting, size of room and furniture all contribute to the sense of intimacy.

- **solid walls** These are very useful when you need to screen out a view, or focus the view in a preferred direction. You can make a solid screening wall more interesting by allowing the wall to start inside the room and continue outside. Using a contrasting material like natural stone or slate will heighten this effect. This is another way of bringing the outside in, adding texture, visual interest and colour.

- **half-glazed walls** These are similar to fully-glazed walls except the window sill is raised from floor-level to form a low wall around the room. The problem here is that you don't have the benefit of enclosure (which a solid wall gives) nor do you have the connection to the garden. However you can make this half-glazed wall work for you by deepening the window sill to create a window-seat. Then you can feel part of the garden and the room at the same time.

design external walls to reflect internal function

the floors can have different levels and finishes which can also be used to define spaces within the open-plan.

- Lowering part of the floor level increases the floor-to-ceiling height and so increases the importance of that space relative to the surrounding spaces (as in the Coast House opposite).

- Raising the floor for a private study area, and adding a small fireplace or window, can create a feeling of intimacy and uniqueness.

- Open-plans within smaller houses are best served by using the same floor material throughout the house to create an illusion of space. However you can still modify the floor material by changing the tiling pattern, or the tile itself, to signify a change in space or function. If using timber, specialist timber floor companies will design and lay your floors, working with different types of timbers, inlays and laying patterns to achieve similar spatial definition.

the living room

The living room will be different things to different people. For some, it will be 'the good room', mainly used for family get-togethers; for others it will be a special place to retreat from the whirl of family life.

sliding walls free up space otherwise constrained by walls and doors. When closed, the sliding walls give a sense of enclosure and intimacy once again

Some people think they have to have a 'good room': an adult-only zone with expensive furniture that is only used once a year. I can almost hear the ticking clock on the mantelpiece! But the living room can be so much more than this. If designed as part of your home – reflecting once again the way you actually live as opposed to how you think you might live – the living room can be the most important space for socialising and relaxing. After all, why put all this expense into a 'good room' that only gets used at Christmas – it would be cheaper to take everyone out on Christmas Day!

To get the most out of your living room, you need to think first about how you could use and enjoy it in different scenarios: relaxing on your own; entertaining family and friends or celebrating with a party.

- **relaxing on your own** One client wanted to be able to watch TV, enjoy the fire, and look out at the view. He told me he hated his living room with a passion because he could only do one of these at any one time. I designed his new house so he could do all three at once using a corner window with an abutting fireplace and adjacent television. Now I'm sure he doesn't know where to look! This three-fold arrangement was so successful that I have replicated it in different ways in many houses since. Everybody wants one!

- **entertaining family and friends** Another client surprised me by saying that he invited around 25 elderly folk to his house after Church for a full Sunday lunch. This may seem an impossible task. But it is perfectly possible to design a home that caters for both the comfort of everyday living and can still expand to be the epicentre of even large family gatherings. One way I do this is by building flexibility into an open-plan arrangement. In the Lough View House opposite, I was inspired by Gerrit Rietveld's 1920s sliding walls which I saw for the first time as a student when I visited his Schröder House in Utrecht.

- **celebrating with a party** A further client was asked by their guest 'did your architect design your house especially for parties?' Although I am not the world's biggest party animal myself, I enjoy designing the ultimate party pad for people who are. I give drama to the open-plan by having at least part of it double height or giving it a cathedral ceiling. I allow some spaces to overlook the main living area; perhaps a landing, a stair gallery or an upper living area. These platforms allow people to retreat a little from the throng below while still enjoying the atmosphere. Finally I open the living room out on to a broad terrace, with huge sliding glass doors to allow the party to flow outside. Here you can set up a band, or have a BBQ going. Seen from the outside, the house then becomes an illuminated backdrop to the party while the outside terrace becomes the stage: an intriguing reversal of roles.

The role of the kitchen in the home is constantly evolving. After the Second World War, something had to be done to make kitchens more attractive to newly-emancipated women who had discovered new roles during the war.

1950s advertising sold the kitchen as a bright, colourful place full of labour-saving gadgets. Designers developed an ergonomic model based on the 'work triangle', which presupposed a single person preparing a meal. This was all appropriate to the era, however, more people are nowadays involved in cooking and the kitchen itself is the focus of a range of activities other than preparing meals. This means that contemporary kitchens are designed in 'zones', which cover both cooking and non-cooking activities.

zone your kitchen according to the activity

cooking zones

- **preparation zone**
  This contains everything you need at hand while preparing and cooking food, including utensils, mixing bowls and spices. You will need a large practical surface to prep your food on.

- **cooking zone**
  This contains everything you need for cooking (ovens, microwaves, stoves, pots and pans).

- **clean-up zone**
  This contains everything you need for washing up after cooking (sinks, dishwasher and recycling bins).

- **consumable zone**
  This contains all your food, including dry, refrigerated and frozen foods. Ideally this should be located in one zone but can work equally well if divided between two areas.

- **non-consumable zone**
  This contains all your crockery, glassware and cookery books.

non-cooking zones

- **communication zone**
  The kitchen has become the hub of the house. In my house, the kitchen island is affectionately known as the 'reception desk' because it is where my children come to log their diary dates with Mum's taxi service. Nowadays it's useful to have a desk area within the kitchen — somewhere to sit and quickly plug in a laptop, update the diary and charge mobile phones.

- **social zone**
  There's nothing worse than being abandoned in the kitchen to cook. Creating a casual seating area, within the kitchen, allows guests and family members to chat with the cooks. This can be a coffee bar that doubles as an informal eating area, or a homework table at other times.

- **utility zone**
  This contains all your laundry equipment. This can be within the kitchen if space is tight. However, to reduce noise from washing and drying machines, it is better to place them in a separate room, or even a small closet.

kitchens are for more than just cooking

Don't panic if your kitchen area isn't large enough to provide a distinct zone for each activity: the essential zones are preparation, cooking and clean-up. All other zones are supplementary. By combining zones in one area you can make your layout multi-task, just as you do.

Kitchen companies vary considerably in both their products and the service they provide and this will be reflected in their prices. At the cheaper end of the spectrum, you can spend £3,000 on a stylish kitchen from a big multi-national, which probably won't last long but you can easily replace it, given the original price. At the other end of the spectrum, you can buy a top-of-the-range kitchen for £30–40,000. If you want this to last you a lifetime, aim for a modern classic that won't date easily. My rule of thumb for what this look might be is that if you can find the same design in a budget outlet, it's already on its way out.

the dining space

Like the kitchen, the dining room should be designed to reflect the dynamics of your family life. This sounds obvious but, in reality, it doesn't happen very often.

Developer homes try to evoke the glory days of English manor houses by locating a separate dining room off the hall. While this was appropriate back then when hosts held glittering candlelit soirées – and had the staff to back them up! – this dining room arrangement doesn't work for most people today. This is why the separate dining room of the developer home is more commonly used as a home study, playroom or extra bedroom. In turn, the family ends up both eating and entertaining in a kitchen that wasn't designed for that dual purpose, and often surrounded by kitchen chaos! Why not design your dining area so it can be used for both everyday use and special occasions?

If you decide to have a dining space within an open-plan kitchen, you need to make it feel special. To do this:

- ensure there is plenty of natural light, by using large areas of glass on the walls to bring sunlight on to the table. Carefully position roof glazing to bring sunlight into north-facing dining areas.
- floor-to-ceiling glass is a must on at least one wall. This draws the eye toward the garden and away from any mess in the kitchen.
- define the dining area and accentuate the table with an unusual, decorative light fitting.

A fireplace will add instant ambience, and warmth, to your dining area. If this is a separate dining room that is used infrequently, a dramatic gas fire built into the wall will provide a convenient and economical solution. For open-plan dining spaces, where the fire will be lit all evening, a freestanding wood-burning stove is better. Choose a stove with a glass door and an external air-vent so that heat from the room is not lost up the chimney.

If you make your everyday dining area a good place to eat you are encouraging your family to share mealtimes. This is all the more valuable in an age when more meals are taken 'on the hoof' than ever – and recent studies show that the typical American teenager spends only 20 seconds in conversation over meals!

make your dining space a beautiful place to enjoy a meal by giving it shape and filling it with light

the bathroom

You might not be able to afford asses' milk and eunuchs waving ostrich-feathers, but there's no reason why your bathroom can't be as individual as you are.

the main en suite bathroom should feel like a special place – somewhere you can relax and feel calm

The contemporary Cleopatra can even design their entire house around their bathroom! One of my clients wanted her bath to look like an infinity-edged pool with a view towards her garden. I wish I'd thought of that! As the old saying goes: never economise on luxuries.

The main en suite bathroom should feel like a special place within your bedroom, somewhere you can relax and feel calm. Depending on your personal preference, the en suite can be anything from hermetically sealed to completely open-plan within the bedroom. The only rule is that it should be spectacular!

Here are some ideas of how to create the stunning bathroom:

- open-plan shower spaces, even big enough for two with dual shower heads, are visually striking, practical for all ages and enhance the feeling of space.
- concealed toilet cisterns allow you to create a seamless look and also makes them easier to clean.
- storage is the key to a successful seamless look. Use floating cabinets with top-mounted basins.
- while aiming for a seamless look, remember the resting eye loves complexity so treat yourself to panels of mosaics, or a section of natural stone.
- double wash-hand basins and sculptural, free-standing, baths make fabulous focus points.
- opaque glass gives you privacy, whilst still allowing natural light.
- heated towel rails will keep your towels dry and warm. But make sure your plumber puts them on a separate circuit so you can time them for bath times.
- use well-lit mirrors to reflect light and double the visual space of your bathroom.
- soaking in the bath is one of life's small pleasures – one bath made for two people with the taps in the middle, is even better. Install a specially designed bathroom TV and stereo speakers to make your stay even longer.

Many clients think every bedroom should have an en suite but remember, as I said before, every bathroom is one that you have to clean! You can reduce the overall number of bathrooms, and still meet your requirements, with careful design. Two children's bedrooms could share an en suite, or all the children's rooms could share one larger, main bathroom with separate toilet.

the bedroom

This is where the magic happens – or can happen if you get the design right!

design each bedroom so the room looks good from the bed

Of all the bedrooms, I position the main bedroom first, so it has a good view and is buffered from potentially noisy areas of the house and site. This is because the main bedroom is not only used for sleeping but is a place to relax. Then I design each bedroom so that it will look good from the bed. Sometimes builders question why I position a small window practically on the floor ("it's so low, I cannae see out"). Of course, it was perfectly positioned to capture the view – but only when you are lying in bed!

the windows If you are a morning person, position the bedroom windows to the south-east so that you can enjoy the morning light. You will probably also love waking up to stimulating colours so decorate your walls with these. If you struggle to get up in the morning choose neutral colours. If you are an evening person, place your windows to the south-west to let in the evening light. Windows on two adjacent walls work wonderfully because you can see the passage of time and changing colours throughout the day.

furniture Like everywhere in the house, it is best to plan the furniture layouts for each bedroom when you design the house. The bed will be the focus of each bedroom so each room should work around the size of each bed anticipated. To make bedrooms restful, keep them free from too much furniture. You should be able to see most of the skirting boards on the walls from the bed – if not, you have too much furniture in the room. Children's rooms should be large enough to accommodate a small double-bed for future flexibility as guest rooms. Children's rooms should be spacious enough to take a small desk area for studying and have enough floor space for a sleepover.

storage Another way of making bedrooms restful is to increase storage space by using built-in wardrobes. These should be flush with the wall and ideally located adjacent to, or behind, the bed, but not facing it. Built-in wardrobes should blend in with the wall – resist the temptation to make a feature of them in any way! If you have a large clothes collection and lots of space, design a walk-in closet off the bedroom. Have it professionally fitted with good lighting and space for a sofa to change on. If you have children of a similar age and gender they might enjoy sharing a walk-in closet with each other – but ask first!

the flooring

With traditional cellular houses, different flooring materials were used in different rooms depending on function. By contrast, open-plan houses use the same flooring material throughout to unify the space.

As with choosing the materials for the exterior of your house, you have a great deal of choice for flooring your interior. Some good choices for the contemporary home are stone, timber, resin and tiles.

stone

choose your flooring material carefully as you will be living with the consequences of your decision for a long time

I love using stone, especially marble and limestone. This gives a softer, more natural and relaxed feel to contemporary interiors. Stone also has the advantage of being available in a range of sizes. By using a range of sizes in the same space, and avoiding uniformity, you can create added visual interest. Stone also comes in a range of finishes, from sand-blasted through to highly polished. You can thus achieve an amazing range of visual effects, while at the same time maintaining continuity by using a single material. With all natural stone, sealing is important. Make sure you obtain a sealant from your stone supplier that doesn't affect the colour or the finish of your stone. You don't want to turn your slate floor shiny or your polished floor matte, so have them demonstrate it for you on a floor sample.

Different stones have different properties:

- marble and limestone are porous materials. So be careful especially with red wine and citrus juice because they will stain your stone easily. I love Jura marble. It contains ammonites, and other prehistoric creatures, which look amazing – and kids love going fossil hunting! The natural colour variations conveniently mean that you don't notice dirty marks. It is also reasonably dense, and therefore hardwearing, and the satin finish has sufficient sheen to produce reflections, without the bother of maintaining a polished floor.
- slate is an excellent choice. I particularly like Welsh slate that has a fairly consistent colour and which comes in either grey/green or blue. Avoid slate that has too much colour variation. Some Chinese slate contains a lot of iron, giving it a black/brown mottled effect, which is not a good contemporary look.
- granite, being very dense, will resist most spilt liquids. It is also very hardwearing. Some people find it rather cold; however, if you are aiming for a sharp, clinical, look, it is ideal.

timber

Timber is a popular choice for many. Its natural variety and colour gives visual warmth to a space and, when used with painted ceilings and glass walls, the effect can be stunning. Timber is also better than carpet for asthma sufferers. If you can obtain the wood from a managed forest, timber is also an ecologically sound option, so this is something you should check in advance.

The species of tree the timber originates from determines its characteristics and qualities. It is therefore important that you ensure your timber is suitable for its intended use, so you should take advice from a specialist supplier. Some timbers vary enormously in how they withstand day-to-day wear. Oak and maple are very hard and are thus suitable for laying in hallways and family living areas. By contrast, walnut is considerably softer, marks more easily, and so is best reserved for special areas, such as a dining space or a library. I once got into trouble for prancing about someone's walnut-floored apartment in my high-heeled boots, giving it the bespoke pock-marked look!

Sunlight also affects the colour of timber over time. For example, if exposed to bright sunlight, walnut turns from dark brown to the colour of light teak in a matter of weeks. You can apply coatings which filter UV light to minimise colour change. In the photo opposite, I used American white oak in the open-plan area because it is hard wearing and retains its colour well.

- the most economical option is a real wood laminate. This is a good choice for children's playrooms and bedrooms where, in the event of disaster, the flooring can be replaced without huge expense.
- a step up from laminate – but still economical – is an engineered board. This is a composite of finished wood, usually on a plywood substrate; the better quality boards can be re-sanded, depending on the thickness of the top wood layer. Both laminate and engineered boards can be laid over underfloor heating
- the most expensive option is, of course, solid wood flooring – which looks and feels fantastic – but bear in mind this is difficult to lay successfully over underfloor heating.

If you have an open-plan living area, it is a good idea to run the timber flooring throughout to give uniformity and maximise the feeling of space. However, if your living area includes a kitchen, minimise the risk of damage to your flooring by locating wet appliances, such as washing machines, in a tiled utility room. If you don't have the space in your house to locate wet appliances separately, you can use a laminate or engineered board to minimise replacement costs if disaster strikes.

if your living space has window walls and timber flooring, use timber decking outside to visually extend the interior space

resin technology

Resin technology flooring uses chemical compounds, which are poured on to the floor to produce a perfectly level and seamless finish. Because there are absolutely no joins in the flooring it was originally developed for use in laboratories and factories, which placed a premium on perfection. In recent years, it has become fashionable – but no less expensive – to use resin technology floors in contemporary homes, especially those at the clinical end of the contemporary design spectrum.

Resin technology has the advantage of making spaces look deceptively large, because there is no jointing, which would otherwise allow the eye to calibrate the size of the space.

The downside to a totally seamless product, however, is that if any part of the floor is chipped or damaged you will have to replace the whole floor, or live with a highly visible patch repair.

tiles

Tiles remain popular because they can accommodate the entire spectrum of contemporary design. If you want the austere, clinical look you can lay 1.2m x 1.2m plain tiles, with narrow joints, to give an almost seamless appearance. Or, you can lay mosaic tiles for a funkier look. Tiles are, of course, durable and most are stain-resistant. They are an excellent choice to lay over underfloor heating because, unlike wood and carpet, tiles are not insulators and so they transfer heat very efficiently from the floor-slab to the room.

There are different types of tiles. Ceramic tiles are made largely from natural, bio-degradable and recyclable materials, in contrast to vitrified tiles, which are made by mixing silica and clay to give a non-porous, glassy look. Ceramic tiles are slightly cheaper than vitrified tiles, however, the latter are more durable and longer lasting.

To make your interior seem as spacious as possible, aim for as few tile joints as possible. You should also try to ensure your grout joint is very narrow and the same colour as your tile. Tiling can be a great way of making a connection between your interior and exterior spaces, for example between a living area, with a window-wall, and a terrace. Using the same tile will draw the eye outside. However, you need to make sure that your interior tile is available in an exterior, non-slip grade. Continuing the tile joints from inside to outside will enhance the visual flow, although it may not enhance your relationship with your tiler!

concrete floors shrink and move more with underfloor heating causing tiles to crack – minimise this by laying a decoupling below the tiles

the lighting

Having ensured that your building possesses the right form and detail, it's now important to get the lighting right as well. Lighting accentuates form and texture.

Lighting is very important both for the interior and exterior of your house.

interior lighting

With interior lighting, there is always a balance to be struck between background ambience, on the one hand, and the need to spotlight features of the room. The role of ambient lighting is to throw light into the room, without drawing attention to the source. It thus creates a soothing atmosphere by providing a soft light to ceilings, walls and floors. Too much calm in a room, however, can be boring and so you also need to include some directional lighting to emphasise, say, a sculpture or a painting, as in the photograph opposite.

use energy efficient 'warm white' bulbs to give a softer feel to your home and reduce your bills

You can also use decorative lighting, such as a show-stopping chandelier to complement your ambient lighting. Decorative lighting is particularly effective over dining room tables, entrance halls and stairs. At the same time there is a balance to be struck here. Too much directional and decorative lighting and your house will quickly look like a nightclub. How many divas do you need on the stage?

exterior lighting

Your house is not a national monument – or, at least, not yet! – so don't floodlight the whole place with orange halogen lamps. The rule with exterior lighting is: less is more.

Highlight the form and texture of your building with ground-recessed up-lighters, which will wash the walls with low-level lighting. Highlight key features of your garden, such as an area of architectural planting or a beautiful tree.

If you use energy efficient LED bulbs you can afford to illuminate your exterior spaces and enjoy them as much at night, from within, as you do during the day.

the interface

Contemporary living connects the inside of the house with the outside. By contrast, traditional houses make a sharp distinction between the inside and outside spaces.

Traditional forms of construction favoured fewer doors and window openings, which also served to protect the inside from the outside, and keep the heat in. Such openings were also somewhat restricted in size, because the traditional lintel could only span a limited distance to support the wall above. Contemporary houses do not share these technological constraints and so the relationship between the inside and outside spaces can be completely different. Modern high-performance doors and windows keep the heat in, while steel lintels allow you to make wider openings in the fabric of the building. All this enables you to unify the relationship between interior living and the external landscape in a way that traditional houses could not.

treat each of your outside spaces as if they are an extension of the house

Here are some ideas of how to design the interface between the inside and outside of your building, drawing together some of my previous thoughts:

- **window-walls** Try to use slim-profile window framing to reduce the visual impact of the frame and increase the visual impact of the view. A sliding or folding door system allows you to physically open up the room completely to the outside space.
- **walls** Extend a feature wall from the inside to the outside through a section of glass. The feature wall could be made of stone, or painted a different colour to the rest of the house.
- **flooring** Extend the same floor material, and preferably the same laying pattern, from the inside to the outside of the house.
- **ceilings** Extend the flow of the ceiling from the inside to the outside, making a covered veranda.

outdoor living

This may seem a little optimistic in our temperate climate, but I still enjoy the odd day when I can breakfast outside with my husband and children and finish off with an impromptu BBQ on the terrace with friends. Even in winter you can enjoy a dry clear night when you can curl up, in a rug, on the garden sofa to enjoy the stars.

By now – and hopefully, following the advice earlier in this book on how to embrace the landscape – you will have already designed your house in such a way that it has interesting spaces around it.

In order to make the most of these outdoor spaces – for there to be meaningful connections between inside and outside – there must be proximity. Make it effortless for you to move from where you are inside to your outside sitting area, for example, by pulling back a big, sliding door and taking your coffee outside to enjoy the sun for half an hour. In the same way, outdoor eating areas need to be handy to the kitchen so that, even if you are cooking inside, you can quickly decide to eat outside without it being a great deal of hassle. Part of making it easy and natural for you to go outside is making it inviting, so think about how your outdoor rooms track the sun. Treat each of your outside spaces as if they were rooms and extensions of spaces within the house.

The main spaces for outdoor living are:

- **outdoor dining** This should be designed either for eating at a particular time of day, or should be in a space that enjoys the sun all day long. To give a feeling of intimacy, and shelter from the breeze, create enclosure by wrapping walls around this space and softening their look with aromatic plants. Trees with overhanging canopies are great, introducing a green ceiling that will reduce the scale of the dining area and make it more inviting.
- **outdoor kitchens** The most luxurious houses today use private gardens to create an amazing compact kitchen that contains everything a regular kitchen has, but is located outside. Originally a Mediterranean idea, it needs a little adaptation for use in our northern climates, but it's nothing a covered veranda and some patio heating can't handle. If you like cooking, but cannot go the length of an outdoor kitchen, build a BBQ or pizza oven into a sculptural, outdoor chimney, either as part of the house design, or as a feature in the garden. Remember to select your flooring material carefully, so it won't suffer from cooking stains.
- **children's play areas** These need to be visible from the kitchen so you can keep an eye on the children. Ideally these play areas should be partly shaded for summer. If you would like a pond but feel you cannot, because of young children, don't give up on your dream. You can construct the pond anyway and just fill it with sand until the children are older.
- **sun terraces** These can be elegant platforms, designed with the grace of an Italian villa and appropriately furnished with sun-loungers and umbrellas, or they can be quiet retreats beneath the dappled shade of a tree. Ideally, aim for both, and give variety to your garden.

choose outdoor furniture that looks good with or without its cushions – that way it can decorate your terrace all year round

3

contemporary lifestyles

contemporary houses for contemporary living
designing for the solo woman
designing for the solo man
designing for families
designing for retirees

contemporary houses for contemporary living

new homes should reflect the way we live today – not a hundred years ago

If you are designing a new home, it makes sense that it reflects the way you live now. So I find it hard to understand why developers insist on providing the traditional four-bedroom, two-reception room, cellular house, that is based on nineteenth-century manor houses, and the strictly hierarchical social structure of that period. Such manor houses had smoking-rooms where the men could talk business while the ladies withdrew to the drawing room. Servants, meanwhile, were banished to the kitchen, which was usually located in the grimmest part of the house. This *Downton Abbey* lifestyle seems completely alien to us now. Yet developers still hark back to this lifestyle as if we, too, can be lords of our own manor. And why have all these – often undersized – cellular rooms, when that isn't how we live today?

That isn't to say, of course, that there is only one sort of contemporary house, or contemporary lifestyle. Far from it. I've worked with over 200 clients over the last 20 years, so I know there are as many different contemporary houses as there are contemporary lifestyles. Nevertheless, similar design issues recur for similar groups of people. So we need to face the challenge of designing contemporary houses that reflect the lifestyles of, variously, the solo woman, the solo man, different sorts of families and retirees.

designing for the solo woman

At the time of writing, over a quarter of all US households now live alone, totalling 33 million Americans.

Professor Eric Klinenberg of New York University, who authored the 2012 study, claimed that 'solitary living is the biggest social change that we have neglected to identify, let alone examine'. A similar trend is emerging in the UK. So we have to think about designing for solo households, remembering all the while that the design needs for the solo woman and the solo man are quite different. In my experience of house design, solo women naturally want their home to express their womanhood. This is reflected in a wide variety of ways but, very often, it's the little things that make the difference:

solo women appreciate womanly homes

- use sofa seating, if space allows, in your open-plan kitchen rather than bar-stools. This will provide a more feminine environment for you and your friends to relax in while cooking.
- the solo woman doesn't have to share her dressing area with anyone! She can have it the way she wants it; professionally fitted and lit. A large walk-in dressing room with bespoke storage for handbags, shoes and clothes, will keep the bedroom clutter-free.
- the solo woman doesn't have to share her bathroom either! So focus on what you really need, depending on whether you are Posh Spice, Sporty Spice or Baby Spice!
- the solo woman may feel, at the end of the day, that she just wants a safe space to curl up in. Make your bedroom a place of Zen calm with a nice fireplace.

Some solo women do not want any overtones in their home of male dominance. This was brought home to me when I was designing a house for a young woman and asked if she had any thoughts about a contemporary over-mantle for the living room fireplace. She shot back: "There'll be no mantle, and there'll be no man leaning on it lording it over my living room." I thought: "Okay. This needs to be a very womanly home." And it was. Other women, who have perhaps experienced divorce, want their home to feel secure. As one client said to me: "This house wraps itself around me – and that's what I need right now." Still others, who have chosen not to have a family themselves, nevertheless want their home to embrace a large extended family. Solo living can still involve catering for large numbers of people.

designing for the solo man

Designing for the solo man presents different challenges to the solo woman.

Perhaps more so than for women, the solo man is more concerned with the impression his home creates on other people. To really work, this impression should be an honest expression of who you really are – and your particular brand of masculinity. A man might be attracted to a look, or a house, that seems 'cool', but if it's not in tune with his personality, there won't be a good fit between him and the house. So think carefully about building materials that really appeal to you and why you find them attractive in a home. For example, if you are an easy-going, nature-loving person, choose tactile materials, such as hand-crafted timber and stone, because these will reinforce your relaxed nature. By contrast, if you are the direct type, you might choose steel, glass and concrete to reinforce your precise and confident nature.

choose a look that best suits your particular brand of masculinity

Here are some ideas I have had when designing houses for the solo man.

- design a good island in the kitchen, with an area for bar-stools. This is great whether you are preparing a meal or having drinks with your mates.
- the solo man doesn't have to share his space with anyone! Memorabilia doesn't have to be consigned to the loft but can be designed into your home from the outset. The champion sportsman can have his trophies displayed in a stunning, walled gallery leading to the living room. A keen reader or academic might have, at the heart of his house, a wonderful double-height library making a fascinating reception area. A classical musician might enlarge a stair landing to take a cello, or carve a shapely recess into the living room to embrace a piano.
- although many men love gadgets and electronics, care is needed when designing them into a beautiful home. Choose one or two attractive pieces per room and integrate them into the purpose of the space. A fabulous stereo and speakers can add to the ambience of the living room, while a sleek computer helps the study appear more stylish.
- design your bedroom as a room just for the bed. Keep technology, such as TVs, stereos and computers to a minimum, using built-in concealed wall units. Keep clothes out of sight, using a walk-in wardrobe.
- men can easily accumulate file boxes, tools and hobby equipment. Plan a heated storage room and fit it out with shelves to handle all these items.
- treat yourself to a gym space and outside jacuzzi, locating both of these close to a shower room for easy access.

designing for families

Most of the houses I design are for people who plan to live in them for the rest of their lives.

The challenge here is to design a house that can adapt, over the decades, to changing family needs. I call this designing for lifetime living. The young couple, starting together, need to think about how the house will work if they have children. I once designed a multi-level, open-plan house for a couple who had been married for many years, without any plans for children. I don't know whether the new house triggered the nest-building instinct, but no sooner were the foundations laid, than the woman announced she was expecting a baby. All I could think of was: 'The Lego will be everywhere!' You also have to think about what will happen when your little cherubs grow into strapping teenagers – often with vast kitbags and giant friends. Finally, you need to consider what happens when your brood have flown the nest (you hope!). How can the house still work when there is just the two of you, again?

design your home for lifetime living

Here are some secrets of designing for lifetime living:

- **design for flexible use** Sometimes it's useful to make a large space smaller, perhaps to safely contain young children or provide a cosier room. Sliding doors that appear miraculously from wall pockets are ideal. They can also work well between an open-plan playroom and family living room, because, when the screens are open, the children can be supervised from the living area, and when the screens are closed they hide the Lego!

- **design for change over time** If you really want a formal dining room, locate it near the kitchen where it can be used as a playroom for young children and, later, a computer room for teenagers – all of whom can be discreetly supervised from the kitchen. When the children leave home, and you have more time for formal entertaining again, this room can revert to its original use. Lofts over garages can initially be used for storage, then a games room for teenagers and, eventually, a hobby room.

- **design for lifetime access** The chances are that someone in your family will have limited mobility at some stage in their lives. This may only be temporary (for example a broken leg) or long-term. The single-storey approach, of course, provides lifetime access to all areas. Alternatively, if you are designing a two-storey house, plan a study/guest bedroom on the ground floor with an adjacent shower room. This means you can accommodate limited mobility without major alterations to the house.

Families come in all shapes and sizes, including blended and home-schooled families.

With separation and divorce, families become more complex and homes should reflect these changing dynamics. There is nothing I enjoy more than the challenge of an unusual brief.

homes today should reflect changing family dynamics

a house for the blended family The first house I designed for two families coming together after divorce involved seven children; aged from toddlers to teenagers. The woman understood that the most important thing for the children, at this time, was for each child to have their own special space. Although the budget was small, I designed the house so that each child had their own unique bedroom – a little balcony for the older children, while others had a bed-loft or a quirky window seat.

a home for the home-schooled family Some years ago I designed a rural house for a family who were home-schooling their children, from nursery all the way through to GSCEs. The whole philosophy of home-schooling is that you receive your education within the home. So I didn't want to take the easy option of designing, for example, a large schoolroom above the garage because the children would still feel they were 'going to school'. I wanted the learning space to be within the home, but this meant I had to overcome the challenge of designing an environment that didn't feel 'half-school, and half-house'. My solution was to design the learning areas into the ground floor where they could open out on to covered terraces and the garden, so some of the learning could take place outside. At the same time I had to design the teaching areas in such a way that they could be incorporated into the home when the children had grown up. To do this I located the learning areas at the heart of the house, where they could later be converted into living spaces.

designing for retirees

Lots of my clients are reaching retirement. Without exception, they have all been fantastic to work for.

I think that's because a pioneering spirit is released with the prospect of a new beginning – which often includes a new home. You may have outgrown the house in which you have raised your family, or you may simply want to resize and start afresh. Whichever, it may be the time when you can, at last, have the house you've always wanted.

If you are upsizing, clearly you have fewer constraints on space and how you use it. If you are downsizing, after a lifetime in a bigger house, there are different design challenges. How can you have a smaller house but not smaller rooms, and what are you going to do with all your furniture? You might want to think about the following:

family heirlooms will work well with your contemporary home provided there is quality in both

- go for an open-plan arrangement, which will give a sense of space. But do define living, kitchen and dining areas carefully so each has character and form.
- introduce vaulted ceilings so even smaller spaces feel generous and airy.
- carefully position glass to visually link interiors with the garden and terrace.
- reduce the number of bedrooms. One main bedroom plus two smaller guest rooms is a better use of space than four bedrooms that are all too small.
- use rooms for more than one purpose: let a guest bedroom double as study.
- be realistic about how many bathrooms you want to clean and plan accordingly. Can guests share an en suite or a main bathroom?
- build in lots of storage that will keep clutter and housekeeping to a minimum.
- you don't need to discard your past. Carefully select key pieces of furniture and art and then design your house around them. Just as in architecture, the old and the new sit comfortably together, providing there is quality in both. For everything else, there are always car boot sales.

4

greening the house

fundamentals of green design

eco standards

insulation

air tightness

ventilation

thermal mass

thermal glass

alternative energy sources

fundamentals of green design

People who want to live in the countryside usually do so because they were born and bred there, or they are simply attracted to its beauty.

Either way, it's not surprising that many clients have a keen sense of environmental responsibility. However, following through on this in a meaningful way – rather than simply making a gesture – involves hard thinking and hard choices. What's the point of building a 9,000sqft house in the country, and then saying it should be built to the highest standards of eco-design? It's an inconsistent position. Similarly, why build a supposedly eco-home, but import your materials from all around the world? Green design is about being green, rather than simply appearing to be green.

So greening your house is about more than just buying all sorts of expensive 'eco-bling' and adding it to your house. Ironically, that could be just another display of consumerism. Rather, greening your house is about making responsible environmental choices based on what you *want* to do, what you *can* do and what you can *afford*. This means that – before we get into the minutiae of sustainable building standards – we should address some fundamentals, chief among which is the need to build modestly and source locally.

make environmental choices based on what you want to do, what you can do, and what you can afford

the modest build Many clients would like a cinema room, a billiard room and an indoor swimming pool – which is fine and I have happily designed such houses. Even though such designs can be offset by appropriate environmental considerations, they will never be 'eco-homes'. If you want an 'eco-home' you need to recognise that this will involve certain constraints from the outset – not least size. An 'eco-home' is not a badge that can be applied post-design. If you truly aim to have a low impact on the Earth's resources, build a modestly-sized home that will suit your needs.

local resources If you want to have a low carbon footprint, source your building components locally. They may cost a little more because local labour costs are higher than in Asia, but you will be acting sustainably while supporting local craftsmen. Remember that sourcing materials locally and purchasing materials locally can be two different things. Materials purchased locally may have travelled further than you think. Once I specified 'Mourne' granite sills from a local supplier, naïvely assuming that the granite was local, when in fact it was quarried and cut in China. Not only was this a bad idea environmentally, it also meant that when things went wrong they took months to fix, because the materials were coming from the other side of the world. So when you purchase your materials locally, check where they are coming from. Doing the right thing, environmentally-speaking, can also be the right thing from a practical point of view.

eco standards

Sweden and Germany, have been at the forefront of advanced building technologies and environmental design for decades. Professors Bo Adamson of Lund University, Sweden, and Wolfgang Feist of the Institute for Housing and the Environment, Germany came up with the idea of a standard for ultra-low energy buildings, which they subsequently developed into the voluntary Passivhaus Standard. This requires your house to meet the following requirements:

- the house must be designed to have an annual heating demand (measured in kilowatt-hours per square metre per year) of less than $15kWh/m^2$ per year in heating and $15kWh/m^2$ per year cooling energy.
- the total energy consumption for heating, hot water and electricity must not be more than $120 \ kWh/m^2$ per year.
- the building must not leak more air than 0.6 times the house volume per hour.

An alternative voluntary standard is that of net zero-energy buildings (ZEB). Such houses aim to use, over the course of a year, less energy than they generate.

> maximise the spaces that you will use every day and be realistic about those that will be used only infrequently

This can be achieved by using solar heating and cooling techniques, along with air-tight construction and super-insulation.

Achieving either a Passivhaus standard or ZEB rating does not come cheap. It will also have massive visual implications for your design. So if you are serious about eco-design to these high standards, you need to be particularly clear about this from the outset – and make sure you can afford it.

Making the right environmental choices for your building will probably mean weighing the following:

- morality – your personal desire to be environmentally responsible.
- aesthetics – the impact of energy-saving devices on the design of your house.
- cost – the initial capital outlay for the energy-saving devices.

There are many different ways in which you can save energy in your home and minimise its carbon footprint. To help you decide what is best for your building, the independent Energy Saving Trust UK (EST UK) will provide the data for costs and savings on all energy-saving devices based on a small three-bedroom, semi-detached house, with standard insulation. While this data is not ideal for the detached rural house, it at least provides an independent basis for comparison.

insulation

Insulating the walls, floor and roof is the most economical way to conserve energy in your home. So my advice is always to make insulation a top priority in your budget. The benefits of insulation are instant, permanent and maintenance-free. Despite this, we still don't insulate enough in the UK and Ireland, compared to Northern Europe.

Most houses in the UK and Ireland are built of masonry. This type of construction suits our northern climate well, in terms of durability and keeping water out, while masonry construction also provides excellent thermal mass, keeping our homes at a more even temperature. However, in an ideal world we would be super-insulating our homes, which means insulating our floors to 300mm, our walls to 400mm and our roof to 500mm. Masonry construction is difficult to insulate to these levels and until these standards are made mandatory, the building industry is not going to change its construction methods to incorporate these requirements. Timber framing, structural insulated panels (SIP) and insulated concrete form (ICF) are alternative ways of constructing and incorporating these high insulation methods.

air-tightness

Now that you have insulated your building you need to ensure heat does not leak out through gaps in the external fabric, such as windows, junctions and electrical conduits. Building Regulations now require houses to be pressure-tested on completion. Houses should not leak more than 10 times their volume per hour. The highest, Passivhaus, eco-standard states that houses should not leak more than 0.6 times their volume per hour but you can achieve around 2.0, or lower, with standard masonry construction, good junction detailing by your architect and traditional craftsmanship, such as wet plastering. Sometimes, if you stand still long enough, technology comes full circle!

ventilation

you can achieve a very air-tight house with traditional construction and craftsmanship

It can be very frustrating when, having gone to all the effort and expense of building an airtight house, you are then required by Building Regulations to provide ventilation in the form of permanent wall vents for fireplaces and trickle vents for windows – all of which can create draughts. There is, however, method in this madness: ventilation is required to bring fresh air into the house and to remove moist air created from your respiration, cooking meals or drying clothes indoors. It is possible to introduce ventilation without draughts by using specialist mechanical ventilating systems that have added heat recovery and which will minimise heat loss.

thermal mass

Thermal mass uses heavy weight construction to absorb heat from the sun during the day and release it slowly during the night. If the glass is orientated towards the sun, you can use natural solar gain to heat your house all year round. If you also have a lot of thermal mass in the building, by using heavy concrete floors and thick masonry walls, excess heat during the summer will be absorbed, effectively cooling the house. This heat is then released at night, warming the house. The overall effect of this is to moderate potential peaks and troughs in temperature.

If your building construction doesn't have thermal mass, such as timber-framed buildings, then you need to prevent your building from overheating during the summer in the first place. You can shade the building by adding louvers, awnings or blinds, or simply by planting deciduous trees. Whichever method you use, it needs to be adjustable to allow the sun to enter in winter and exclude it in the summer. Alternatively, you can add thermal mass to a timber-framed building using the space-age Phase Change Material (PCM): where wax-based products are incorporated within a construction board and applied to walls and ceilings to absorb, then release, excess heat.

thermal glass

In contemporary houses, glass is the key element to connecting the interior space with the landscape. It used to be that a lot of glass meant a lot of heat loss but, with advances in technologies, this should no longer be the case. The rate at which heat is lost through a material is called its U-value, which is measured in watts per square metre per degree Kelvin (W/m2K). The lower the U-value, the less heat is lost. A reasonable U-value to expect from good quality thermal double-glazing is around 1.2 W/m2K. By contrast, a two-foot thick stone wall has a U-value of 1.68W/m2K. So, ironically, a contemporary house with thermal double-glazing will actually lose less heat than a traditional stone cottage. If you think that is impressive, triple-glazing with krypton gas and insulated frames will bring the U-value of your windows down to an incredible 0.8 W/m2K. Unfortunately, such glazing systems are still very expensive and the payback period, for the amount of energy saved, is very long.

If you install thermal double-glazing, the internal surface temperature (IST) at the window when it is really cold outside will be around 16°C. This is a reasonable level of comfort and a big improvement on a single-glazed window (where the IST will be around 1°C) and a standard double-glazed window (where the IST will be around 11°C). However, if you install a thermal triple-glazed window the IST is around 18°C – not much improvement on 16°C but very much more expensive. Despite this, should you decide to go for thermal triple-glazing, ensure it is manufactured locally. Waiting ten weeks for replacement glass to arrive after someone has put a scaffolding pole through your window will not endear you to the product – no matter how good its U-value.

alternative energy sources

With oil prices continuing to rise, it is prudent to look at other ways of heating your house. Even the most eco-friendly houses need some source of heating in winter – even if it is just a log-burning stove. You also need to think about your domestic hot water demands which cannot be met by solar panels alone.

air source heat pumps

Air source heat pumps are powered by electricity. They extract heat from outside air and absorb this, at low temperatures, into a fluid. This is then compressed to produce a higher temperature that in turn heats the home. The advantage of these pumps is that they can operate in all temperatures, even as low as -15° C. Such pumps need space and are most efficient when placed on a south-facing wall, with plenty of airflow. Air source pumps heat to a lower temperature than boilers, so your home needs to be well insulated for these pumps to be effective.

contemporary houses are potentially ideal for exploiting solar gain because they incorporate a lot of glass into their design

Types of air-source heat pumps:

- **air-to-water** This is linked to your water-based heating system. It works best with underfloor heating because of the lower water temperature requirements.
- **air-to-air** This produces warm air which is distributed around the house using fans and ducts.

wind turbines

There are two types of wind turbines for domestic use: high-output turbines which are pole-mounted, and low-output turbines which are building-mounted.

Once again, if you are in a 'feed-in' tariff area you can sell any excess electricity back to the National Grid, reducing your payback period. If you are not in a 'feed-in' tariff area, you can store unused electricity in batteries for use on a calm day. Batteries are expensive, however, and every time you change the electricity from one form to another, efficiency drops drastically.

hydroelectricity

If you have a stream, or river, on your site then, subject to permission from the relevant environment agency, you may be able to harness the energy of the water, using a small hydro-power system. Your water source needs to have the right combination of 'head' (the difference in height over a short distance) and 'flow' (the rate at which the water flows per second). For example, a water source that has a lot of flow but a small head (such as the flow of water over a dam) is unlikely to have enough energy to create electricity. In any case, you will need advice from a specialist supplier who will take flow readings. The payback period of the hydro power system will entirely depend on how long the turbine will run and produce electricity, and whether or not you are in a 'feed-in' tariff area.

biomass boilers

Biomass boilers are specialised units that burn non-fossil fuels to produce heat. Because all plant life produces CO_2 as part of its normal cycle of decay, the burning of non-fossil fuels is not deemed to be adding to the CO_2 in the atmosphere as it is going to end up there at some stage anyway.

If you own land and can grow willow for burning, a biomass boiler is a very economical prospect provided you don't mind a bit of hard labour at the weekends. You can also run the biomass boiler using manufactured pellets, which are currently cheaper than heating oil – but ensure that the pellets are locally manufactured as imported pellets may not be as green as you think.

Biomass and pellet boilers are more expensive than a high-efficiency, oil-fired, condensing boiler and they require more maintenance. At the very least you should have a biomass boiler that is fully automated both in terms of cleaning and refuelling. You will also need to provide housing for both the boiler and the receptacle for the pellets so that you can bulk order pellet supplies. This too carries a cost and should be factored into the payback period of the biomass boiler.

if using manufactured pellets with a biomass boiler, ensure they are manufactured locally, as imported pellets may not be as green as you think!

solar panels

Two types of solar panels are commonly in use: photovoltaic and hot water solar panels.

- **photovoltaic solar panels** use photovoltaic (PV) cells to generate electricity. This free electricity can be used to heat your house and the excess electricity can be sold back to the National Grid if you are in what is called a 'feed-in' tariff area. England, Scotland and Wales have 'feed-in' tariffs whereas Northern Ireland has no feed-in tariff areas, and in the Republic of Ireland it is left to each supplier to agree a tariff or not. This is a problem for homes in Ireland because you can only benefit from the free electricity you generate by using it and you give any excess back to the National Grid for free. This radically affects the payback period of your solar panels, lessening the incentive to use them.
- **hot-water solar panels** are plumbed into the hot water cylinder and provide hot water in the summer months. In winter, when there is less sun, the water needs to be heated by other means, such as your boiler or immersion heater. This in turn affects the payback period of these solar panels.

underfloor heating with ground source heat pumps

Underfloor heating warms the whole floor, usually with water-filled pipes embedded in the floor. Radiant heat is emitted, like the heat from the sun, and is absorbed uniformly by all the other surfaces in the room – including your walls and furniture – which, in turn, become secondary heat emitters and heat reflectors. The net effect of this is to create an evenly-heated environment, without cold spots. It also means that you do not have to make much allowance for the height of the room because, with radiant heat, the temperature of the room actually reduces as the height increases, so it is perfect for heating spaces with cathedral ceilings. This method contrasts with radiators because they transfer heat into a room largely by convection, leaving the floor as the coldest part of the room and the ceiling the warmest.

Underfloor heating uses lower temperature water than radiators and so ground source heat pumps are a good alternative energy source because they too work on lower temperatures. The ground source heat pump works by drawing low-grade heat from large volumes of water, which are pumped around the garden, and converts it into smaller volumes of high-grade heat, which is then pumped around the house. Ground source heat pumps are relatively expensive to install. If there is a leak in one of the underground pipes, they are not easy to access for repair. Depending on the insulation of your house, you may have to boost the heat in the floor to make your house warmer. Because boosting the heat uses electricity, this will reduce the efficiency of the system and in turn affect the payback period.

Other benefits of underfloor heating are:

- it is safe, unobtrusive and frees up wall space.
- It is virtually maintenance-free.
- It does not create the same levels of dust as radiators or hot air systems.
- It reduces levels of humidity in floor coverings and reduces dust mites.
- It reduces air movement and so helps create a low allergy environment, by reducing the ingress of fungi spores.
- It's also much appreciated by pets!

up until now the team has just been you and your architect,
but it's about to get a whole lot bigger

– about this big!

5

the suppliers

compiled by
Claude Costecalde

Lagan Building Solutions (LBS)

In 2007 we acquired four of the last remaining slate quarries in north Wales, which included the world famous Penrhyn quarry. Penrhyn slates, commonly referred to by the name Bangor Blue, have been coming into Ireland for the last 600 years, and they are the ultimate roofing slate in terms of both quality and appearance.

When we were asked to specify slates for the Lough View House, there was only one slate that could meet the clients' requirements: Bangor Blue. The house, with its vast, dominant roofs sheltering glass and stone pavilions beneath, needed a slate roof that had consistency in quality and colour. High quality slates lay better because their thickness and flatness are uniform throughout. This gives the roof a homogenous look, which suits a contemporary house. The Bangor Blue slates on the Lough View House give a sharp, contemporary look using a traditional, rural material.

Bangor Blue slates are easily recognised by their unique heather blue or purple colour, and typically have a lifespan of anywhere between 150–300 years. Although most famous as a roofing material for some of the world's most prestigious houses, it is also becoming increasingly popular for other architectural applications such as walling and building stone, paving and flooring tiles, window sills, lintels and fireplace hearths and surrounds.

There are many types of roofing products on the market, and choice can be guided by economy as well as quality and colour. We select the best slates from quarries around the world, as well as clay roof tiles from the leading international manufacturers.

There are also many types of walling products on the market. Our natural stone panel system, Z Stone, is available in black slate, multi-coloured slate, quartz and granite, and works well when building on a limited budget.

Bangor Blue slates gave this house a sharp contemporary look using a traditional rural material

Ballycastle Homecare Ltd

Bathroom design has blossomed in the past ten years, and, for the contemporary home, the bathroom is now a key area to indulge your design fantasies. We work with Ireland's leading architects to produce stunning bathrooms in the most forward looking, designer homes. Only by embracing design opportunities, presented by challenging projects, can your skills as a designer grow, and this is what makes our business such an exciting place to be.

Ours is a small family business, located in the picturesque town of Ballycastle, on the north coast of Ulster. It began thirty years ago, and has grown to become one of Ireland's leading retail bathroom showrooms.

Design is at the heart of our business, and, since Germany leads the way in both bathroom product and bathroom design, we have been selected to exclusively carry the German, award-winning, Dornbracht range in Northern Ireland, and additionally their sister range from Alape. We also carry other leading German brands such as Duravit, Hansgrohe and Villeroy & Boch. Complementing these product ranges, we have our own joinery workshop and a team of skilled cabinet-makers. These on-site facilities allow us to tailor each bathroom with bespoke furniture, so making every project unique.

Parkes Interiors

Today's contemporary kitchens are the ultimate multi-taskers – and the new heart of the home. At Parkes Interiors, we specialise in designing dynamic open-plan spaces where you can cook, eat, relax and entertain. The Hayfield House and the Bawn House were two such projects. With beautiful, bespoke, German kitchens we used complementary woods, and cool laminates, to define activities, yet provide a seamless look throughout both kitchens.

Based in Belfast, since 1993, the design studio and its director, Brian Parkes, have won many industry awards including: Top Kitchen Retailer Ireland, Top kitchen Designer Ireland and Top Kitchen Showroom UK. We keep innovation at the top of our agenda by continuing to develop close working relationships with our German manufacturing partners. Europe is leading the way in terms of cutting-edge design, materials and products. So it gives us enormous pleasure to bring these innovations to our clients in the UK and Ireland – even when working on a traditionally styled kitchen. To help you, and us, visualise how the finished interior will look and feel, we use the latest 3d walk-through technology. This helps bring the design to life, in all its detail and spatial effects.

Geddis

In the past thirty years of running our family business, we have seen enormous developments in fireplace design and functionality. Much of this is environmentally driven, and today we stock many high-efficiency, log and bio-fuel, stoves from leading manufacturers in Denmark, Belgium and Italy. These include Hwam, Morso, Nestor Martin and Palazzetti.

Alternatively, gas fires are a convenient and very popular choice, particularly for those intermittently used spaces of the home, such as dining rooms, halls and bedrooms. In Wilmont Cottage, Belfast, we used a magnificent gas Faber 'Relaxed' model in a large format, which both visually commanded the large open-plan space, whilst giving the correct heat out-put.

Whether your fire appliance is a stove, a gas fire or a traditional fireplace, choose the right fireplace to give an entertaining space, an unrivalled focus, or a bedroom, a luxurious ambience.

Your chosen fireplace should also be selected to suit the function of the room, and the size of space it needs to heat. You don't want your living space to be under-heated, or your sleeping space over-heated. At our designer showrooms in Lisburn, Northern Ireland, our experienced team of designers and technical experts will be able to advise which fire appliance will best suit your space, and you.

David Scott Tile and Stone

The 'Tile Refinery' is our award winning showroom located in the heart of Belfast city centre. In it, we feature an incredible range of leading brands from around the world, showcasing them in large room-settings to let you experience what the products will look like in your own home.

Although we can spoil you with choice with the latest designs, and traditional products, we will carefully consider the architecture of the building first, before advising what tiling might complement it. When we were asked to do the tiling for the Origami House, and similarly the Lough View House, we realised that the architecture (highly sculpted ceilings and glazed walls) was going to be extremely powerful. If a lot of detail was added to the floor-tiling, it would only detract from the spatial experience. In our view, if the architecture is the melody then the flooring should be its beat. We suggested Jura limestone because this natural material would provide a consistent colour tone with just enough visual variation, coming from its fossils, to provide relief without being a distraction.

It has been a great privilege to have worked on many of Ireland's most significant landmark buildings including The Titanic Signature Building and our own award-winning house, 'Scotts on the Rocks'. We have been voted 'Leading Independent Retailer' twice by Belfast City Council and 'Best Independent Retailer in Great Britain and Ireland' by The Tile Association (TTA).

We are proud to be a family owned and run business, and, whatever your design, we have two generations of experience here to help you make the right choices for your project.

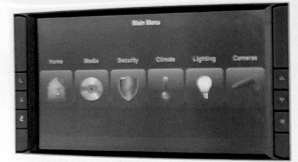

Main Menu

Home   Media   Security   Climate   Lighting   Cameras

Indigo Distribution

We are surrounded by technology in our homes: smart TVs, smart phones, web tablets, cloud services, media streaming, anything Apple – the list is endless. All this home-technology makes life easier for some and more confusing for others. We work closely with your professional technology installer, your architect and your electrician to make sure your home-technology works together and is simple for anyone to use.

We design, supply and support digital home solutions from the world's leading electronic companies. Our solutions are simple to use with the music sounding great in any room and the high definition television making movies look amazing.

When designing your new home, or when renovating your existing home, it is important to plan ahead. So, from the outset of design, think about how you will live with the technologies in your home:

- Where, for instance, will you watch TV, listen to music or enjoy home cinema?
- Integrate music, television, Internet, lighting, heating and security systems into a single, simple to use solution that can be operated securely, anywhere in the home or when you are across the globe.
- Specify only electronic equipment that can be linked together and operated with one easy-to-use control system.
- Wire for everything, as even wireless applications need wires.

Home technology is a rapidly evolving world, so it is important to talk to a professional technology installer who understands the possibilities. We will work with you and your installer to ensure that you get the digital solution that is right for you.

it's never too early to think about the home-technology for your new house, so that it blends seamlessly with the design

with open-plan,
double-height spaces,
use underfloor heating
to give a consistent
room temperature

BM Heat Services Ltd

Energy conservation is now a top priority for architects and house builders. As a result, the design of heating and ventilating systems, in order to maximise energy efficiency, have become increasingly technical. As manufacturers' agents, we provide the technical and practical support needed during the design process, on-site installation, and beyond.

With so many systems on the market, the self-builder is faced with an array of options: high-output radiators, under-floor heating, heat recovery units, solar thermal panels, and ground or air-source heat pumps. However, some technologies will work better together than others, depending on the design of your house. The floor area, ceiling heights, insulation levels, areas of glazing and orientation will all affect the way your house should be heated, and the air distributed through it. Additionally, not all heating, heat recovery and renewable energy systems work efficiently with one another in all houses. As a supplier of all these systems, under one roof, we can help you integrate these systems to maximise energy efficiency and reduce your energy bills.

For the Holestone House, we chose a weather compensated under-floor heating system for the open-plan, double-height, ground floor spaces (to give a consistent room temperature throughout the living spaces), combined with radiators for the first floor bedrooms (to allow flexibility of temperature in the first floor sleeping spaces). Double format solar panels were then added in as a renewable source for hot water heating.

In our Radiator Shop, a dedicated designer showroom in Newtownards, we are able to showcase the latest styles from the world of designer heating.

PM Lighting

We all know what good lighting is – but unfortunately only when we see it! Lighting is a fundamental component in every good design. It is the quality of this light that distinguishes good lighting design from bad, and so, at PM Lighting, we specialise in light that makes the space within and around your home more beautiful.

As consultants and suppliers of specialist interior lighting, we have a wealth of experience in home, office, hotel and restaurant projects. Each interior has its own distinctive requirements, overlaid by your personal design brief. Our extensive, and exclusive, range of lights from around the world will perfectly complement your design, creating a unique atmosphere that perfectly reflects your personality and needs.

Exterior lighting can enhance the beauty of your home, and will improve both safety and security. For contemporary houses, such as the Origami House, exterior lighting can add an atmospheric dimension to the setting of the house, or lend a dramatic back drop to the interior spaces.

Park Engineering

My late father, Alec Park, started our metal-working business 60 years ago from a small workshop on the family farm in Ballymena, Northern Ireland. He had a great pair of hands, and a good eye for detail, so the business quickly grew from agricultural machinery to the design and manufacture of bespoke gates and railings. We still use my father's anvil, fire and hammer (which itself is over 100 years old) to shape, by hand, anything our high-tech metal rollers and bar scrollers can't manage!

Our core products are railings and gates (which are now mostly automated). Quality and reliability are paramount with automatic gates, so we use automation systems from DEA, who were among the first in Europe to define this new field of engineering. Today, in more modern surroundings than my father enjoyed, we also make to special order: spiral staircases, garden furniture, and even street lights and street furniture. It is wonderful to be able to make products for all kinds of properties, from private houses to public hospitals.

Roskyle Ltd

We thrive on challenges and few projects are more challenging than modern extensions to Listed Buildings. Here, the quality of the new-build needs to match, and ideally exceed, the quality of the existing – but using contemporary materials. The key to success is attention to detail. One such project was Wilmont Cottage, Belfast. This was a cutting-edge, white rendered and glass extension to the rear of a terraced, brick cottage. The architect's idea was that the extension would be a room within a contemporary walled garden, overlooking the estate-land beyond. On this build, we dedicated an expert foreman to the project, along with a team of specialist craftsmen, to work with the client, the architect, and Historic Buildings Branch, and ensure that every detail was delivered to perfection.

Other projects present structural challenges such as: the twisted, stepped, form of the Lough Beg House; or the two-storey, stepped, form of the Hayfield House. In these two projects, we used a computerised steel-manufacturing system to design, measure, cut and prefabricate a complete steel frame to fit precisely inside, what would become, the exact form of the building.

We work for many clients, throughout the UK and overseas, who want to have the self-build experience but also want to avoid the stress of hiring direct-labour and managing their own build process. Equally, our clients want to be assured that their new distinctive home will be completed to the highest standards, and we pride ourselves in having the skills and commitment to achieve that.

Andrew Hamilton Construction

The Origami House was an exciting build for us because it was so different. The internal folded ceiling, with its numerous junctions ending in precise corners floating in space, may look effortless now, but they weren't at the time! The only way to deliver such perfection is to have dedicated leadership and a team of highly skilled craftsmen all willing to work towards the one goal – perfection. This wonderful house has won numerous awards, which has given us the opportunity to work on many contemporary houses since.

We value traditional building skills and believe in sustaining our local labour force. My team is therefore made up of local men with whom, over the past twenty years, I have forged strong working relationships. This is our key to delivering precision and quality.

MG Construction

In 25 years of building, the Lough View House is by no means the biggest house we've built – but it was one of the most challenging. One such aspect was getting the stonework right. The huge stone chimneys on the front of the house, and the high curved retaining wall forming the rear courtyard, put the architectural focus on the stone. We looked at many types of stone by various suppliers and stonemasons. We had to consider quality, durability, colour, laying patterns, and availability of the stone in large quantities. We then constructed various sample panels so that the architect, and clients, could approve the way forward.

We give this level of attention to detail to each of our projects – whether that's a small cottage, a country mansion, or a commercial enterprise – and bring to the job a wealth of building, and product, experience.

Noel Savage Construction Ltd

Running a family business, with over 100 years of building experience between us, allows us to get involved in projects that make a difference to our environment: preserving our built heritage, constructing new schools and renewing our residential stock. One such project was the innovative, and environmentally conscious, Holestone House. The trickiest part of the build was the double-height, oak-framed, interior. This space also had sliding, glazed, oak doors that could divide the ground floor open-plan into separate kitchen, dining hall and living spaces. Oak is difficult to work with because it can be unstable. So we had to carefully monitor the moisture levels in both the timber and the environment into which it was going. Our skilled craftsmen designed and engineered the oak frames into sleek models of contemporary perfection!

Murphy Joinery Ltd

We established our joinery-works, situated on the beautiful shores of Lough Neagh, Northern Ireland, to meet, in particular, the demands of leading contemporary architects who are pushing the boundaries of timber door and window design.

Sliding timber doors, such as those on the Hayfield House and the Lough Beg House, can be used to great dramatic effect: to blur the boundaries between inside and outside; or to provide flexible division within larger open-plan spaces.

Fundamentally, we are interested in architectural design and we love bringing our skills, technical knowledge and understanding of timber, to all sorts of projects from self-builds to award-winning properties.

B&C Surveys

Digital surveying is the vital link between the site, the design, construction and landscaping. At the outset, we provide the architect with a 3D electronic drawing of the site including contours, trees, boundaries, waterways, existing buildings and services. This is the base drawing for the project, allowing the architect to then design their building into the site. The resulting combined survey and architect's drawing is then used by the contractor to accurately price the work keeping cost over-runs for unforeseen work to a minimum. When the building work commences, we return to site and digitally set the building out. I remember when the contractor for the Origami House asked us to set out a 'bungalow in Kells', I assumed I was going to plot four corners – I got a bit of a shock when there were, in fact, thirty two!

Hortus Tuus – Keith Crawford

My aim is to make each garden special. As a horticulturalist and radio broadcaster, I love working with plants, and working with people – to make a good garden, I believe, you need to be in tune with both.

At the Springhill House, we augmented the existing mature trees with hard-landscaping, and planting, to draw the eye and frame the lake views. At the Lough View House we used architectural planting on the terraces to create stunning shapes and textures within a tight colour-palette. By contrast, at the Origami House, we lined the banks of a waterway with bog plants to give year-round colour and visual interest. Sensitive design, good site preparation, and quality plants will produce a garden guaranteed to bring lasting pleasure.

conclusion

Finally the builders, with all their diggers and debris, have gone. The house is clean and quiet – yours at last!

When I arrive for the handover, I never walk right into the house, but instead ring the doorbell. Having been responsible for every nook and cranny of the build, I am now pleased to feel more like a guest. This is, after all, the point of the journey, which began with a mood board and has ended with a house that will enable my clients to live the way they'd envisaged.

For my clients, it's a time of celebration and excitement, although for me, it's tinged with a little sadness because the particular journey we've been on is now over. It is, however, the start of a whole new chapter. The house is now a home. I love going back to see my clients when the rooms are all furnished, their paintings released from storage, and the house is a full flowering of their personalities, as it was always meant to be.

Some of my clients' friends have told them that you have to build four houses before you get your dream house right. But, in fact, if you think your way through every aspect of the design, there's no reason why you can't get your dream house right first time. My hope is that this book will equip you, and your architect, to do just that – to achieve your vision and create a beautiful piece of architecture in the process. You too can master the art of building a house in the countryside, and, in doing so, enhance our landscape for generations to come.

Jane

acknowledgements

To my publisher Dr Claude Costecalde of Booklink, I am indebted for his vision and guidance, without which this book would still be on my bucket list.

Thanks go also to my brother, Professor Jonathan Burnside, who patiently translated my ideas into a language I hope you can understand.

To my photographer, Chris Hill, who has been photographing my work for over twenty years, I thank you for persevering through snow-storms and heat-stroke to get the perfect shot!

My appreciation goes to Wendy Dunbar for this beautiful book design and her fastidious attention to detail.

Special thanks go to my husband, David, for his unwavering support and encouragement; to my Mum and Dad for giving me such a good start in life; and to my two sons, Ryan and Chris, for reminding me that I had a book to write, when the sofa was more tempting.

Many professional colleagues have helped me deliver these beautiful houses: my quantity surveyor, Jim Carlisle (complete with Mont Blanc pencil), ensures that all my projects come in on budget; my structural engineers, Richard Nicholl, George Coulter, David Clements, and Jonathan McCauley, manage to design steelwork that is almost invisible; and my office colleagues, both past and present (in particular Charlie Cooke) who have detailed these houses so beautifully.

The Planning Service plays an important role in both the protection and development of our landscape. So my thanks goes to the planning officers for recognising the value creative design can have in contributing to the beauty of our landscape.

For shaping my thinking: first as a student, I am indebted to Prof. Patrick Hodgkinson and Peter Aldington; as a practitioner, I wish to thank Hugh Newell Jacobsen and the late Geoffrey Bawa for their inspirational work.

Contemporary Design Secrets is based on the many conversations I have shared with clients during the making of their wonderful homes. It has not been possible to feature all the houses, or extensions to houses, I have completed over the twenty-year span of my work. However, every house is inherently embodied in this book because each project shapes the next. So my final thank you is for my clients who took that initial leap of faith and allowed me to deliver their dream.

Lagan Building Solutions Ltd (LBS)
Sheepwalk Road
Lisburn, Co. Antrim, BT28 3RD
Tel: +44 (0) 28 9264 8691
Fax: +44 (0) 28 9264 8935
www.LBSproducts.com
E-mail: info@LBSproducts.com

Ballycastle Homecare
2 The Diamond, Ballycastle
Co. Antrim, BT54 6AW
Tel: +44 (0) 28 2076 2311
Fax: +44 (0) 28 2076 2418
E-mail: info@ballycastlehomecare.co.uk

Parkes Interiors
302 Upper Newtownards Road
Belfast BT4 3EU
Tel: +44 (0) 28 9020 9209
Fax: +44 (0) 28 9020 2254
E-mail: sales@parkesinteriors.co.uk

Geddis Fireplaces,
Portman Business Park,
Rathdown Road,
Moira Road,
Lisburn.
Tel: +44 (0) 28 9262 1011
www.geddisfireplaces.co.uk

David Scott Tiles Ltd
The Tile Refinery
11–19 Blythe Street
Sandy Row, Belfast, BT12 5HU
Tel: +44 (0) 28 90232136
Fax: +44 (0) 28 90 438611
E-mail: Info@davidscotttiles.com

Indigo Distribution
92 Dunlop Commercial Park
Balloo Link, Bangor
Co. Down, BT19 7HJ
Tel: +44 (0) 28 9145 5565
Fax: +44 (0) 28 9185 9875
Mob: 7799 801 901
www.indigodistribution.ie

BM Heat Services Ltd
Scrabo Business Park
Jubilee Road, Newtownards
Co. Down, BT23 4YH
Northern Ireland
Tel: +44 (0) 28 9181 3460
    +44 (0) 28 9181 5991
Fax: +44 (0) 28 9181 9909
E-mail: info@bmheat.com
www.bmheat.com

PM Lighting
Scrabo Business Park
Jubilee Road, Newtownards
Co. Down, BT23 4YH
Northern Ireland
Tel: +44 (0) 28 9181 3460
    +44 (0) 28 9181 5991
Fax: +44 (0) 28 9181 9909
E-mail: info@bmheat.com
www.bmheat.com

Park Engineering
35 Duneaney Road
Glarryford, Ballymena
Co. Antrim, BT44 9HP
Tel: +44 (0) 28 2568 5374
Mob: 07808 931574
E-mail: parkduneng@aol.com

Roskyle Ltd
32 Plantation Street
Killyleagh, Co Down, BT30 9QW
Tel: +44 (0) 28 4482 8229
Fax: +44 (0) 28 4482 8755
E-mail: info@roskyle.co.uk
www.roskyle.com

Andrew Hamilton Construction
180 Carnlough
Ballymena, Co. Antrim, BT43 7JW
Tel: +44 07712 873 346
Fax: +44 (0) 28 256 84555
E-mail: andy@acornhomes.co.uk

MG Construction
3 Ballytrustan Road
Downpatrick, Co. Down, BT30 7AQ
Tel: +44 (0) 28 4484 1368
E-mail: info@mgconstruction.com
www.mgconstruction.com

Noel Savage Construction Ltd
98B University avenue,Belfast,BT7 1GY
Tel: +44 (0) 28 9032 1080
Mob: 07771812469
info@noelsavageconstruction.com

Murphy Joinery Ltd
51 Moss Road
Magherafelt, Co. Derry, BT45 6LJ
Tel: +44 (0) 28 79 418881
Fax: +44 (0) 28 79 418903
E-mail: info@murphyjoinery.com
www.murphyjoinery.com

Robert Boyd T/A B&C Surveys
42 Paisley Road
The Commons, Carrickfergus, BT38 9AH
Mob: 07751249479
E-mail robert.bcs@btinternet.com

Hortus Tuus
25 Shandon Park, Belfast, BT5 6NW.
Tel: +44 (0) 28 90704670
Fax: +44 (0) 28 90704671
Mob: 07810051108
E-mail: keith@hortustuus.co.uk

Jane D. Burnside Architects
Origami House
14 Whappstown Road
Kells, Ballymena, BT42 3NX
Tel: +44 (0) 28 25892658
E-mail: janeburnside@aol.com

Published by Booklink
www.booklink.ie
Publisher: Dr Claude Costecalde, Booklink
© Text, Jane Burnside 2012
© Photographs, Chris Hill
© Design, Booklink, 2012
Design, Wendy Dunbar
ISBN 978-1-906886-42-4